ECONOMIC ACTIVITIES OF CHILDREN : DIMENSIONS, CAUSES AND CONSEQUENCES

Economics Activities of Children: Dimensions Causes and Consequences

– by –
B. M. DINESH

2018
Daya Publishing House®
A Division of
Astral International Pvt. Ltd.
New Delhi - 110 002

First Published, 1988
Reprinted, 2018

ISBN: 978-81-7035-040-8 (Hardbound)

Publisher's note:

Every possible effort has been made to ensure that the information contained in this book is accurate at the time of going to press, and the publisher and author cannot accept responsibility for any errors or omissions, however caused. No responsibility for loss or damage occasioned to any person acting, or refraining from action, as a result of the material in this publication can be accepted by the editor, the publisher or the author. The Publisher is not associated with any product or vendor mentioned in the book. The contents of this work are intended to further general scientific research, understanding and discussion only. Readers should consult with a specialist where appropriate.

Every effort has been made to trace the owners of copyright material used in this book, if any. The author and the publisher will be grateful for any omission brought to their notice for acknowledgement in the future editions of the book.

Published by : **Daya Publishing House**®
A Division of
Astral International Pvt. Ltd.
– ISO 9001:2008 Certified Company –
4736/23, Ansari Road, Darya Ganj
New Delhi-110 002
Ph. 011-43549197, 23278134
E-mail: info@astralint.com
Website: www.astralint.com

FOREWORD

This is a study carried out by Late Shri B.M. Dinesh as a student at the Institute for Social and Economic Change during 1979-84 under my supervision and guidance. Before he could appear for the *viva-voce* examination in order to complete the formalities for the award of the Ph.D. degree by the University of Mysore, he was snatched away from this world in an unfortunate accident in July, 1986. In his premature death, I feel we have lost a promising researcher and academician. Those who had gone through the earlier draft of this manuscript had very favourably evaluated the same. Many of my colleagues at the Institute felt that this study had made an important contribution to the existing literature on the topic and they have persuaded me to publish it with suitable modifications in the text.

The theme for this work is rooted in the micro economic theory of fertility as the starting point for considering the contribution of children to the household economy in a rural setting. Noting the availability of only a few fragmentary pieces of information on the topic, the study focusses on the dimensions, causes and consequences of economic activities of children. It has also attempted to study the compatibility of schooling and work and understand the parents' perception of the importance of the economic contribution of children. The primary data have been gathered from three selected villages of Dakshina Kannada district of Karnataka state.

Children in the school going ages (6-15 years) have been

grouped into four mutually exclusive categories according to school-work status, *viz.* (1) those who go to school but do not work, (2) those who go to school and also work, (3) those who work but do not go to school, and (4) those neither go to school nor work. Dimensions of child work participation have been gauged in terms of (a) magnitude of work, (b) intensity of work, (c) place of work, (d) nature of activities performed, and (e) the wages earned. For the purpose of analysing the causes of child work participation a bivariate classification of children has been made by taking the percentage of children in each work-school status category by background variables such as land ownership, education, number of siblings, caste and religion, etc. Similarly consequences of participation of children in work to their contribution to family income, school attendance, their performance in school, etc. have been analysed.

The findings of the study have implications for theory as well as for policy. The economic contributions of children have to be understood in terms of current and future utility to their parents. The findings indicate that current and future utility vary by their school work status and have very important implications on the decision-making of couples. Also the findings of the study suggest that any policy measures to improve the schooling rate of children particularly in the rural areas of the country should take into account the current economic utility of children to their parents discounted for the future.

In this endeavour of editing the work and its publication I have received generous help from many quarters. Prof. V.M. Rao and Mr Syed Ajmal Pasha have rendered much help at the time of editing the manuscript. The Indian Council of Social Science Research, New Delhi was generous enough to award a publication grant for its publication. Those who were particularly helpful in this endeavour were Prof. Amitabh Kundu, Shri Kashmiri Singh, and Prof. G.M.K. Madnani who evaluated the work for ICSSR and made useful suggestions which have been incorporated in the revised version. Finally, the Daya Publishing House, Delhi have brought this volume in a record time. For all of them I owe a debt of gratitude.

Institute for Social
and Economic Change,
Banglore, 560 072

P. HANUMANTHA RAYAPPA
(Professor and Head
Population Research Centre)

ACKNOWLEDGEMENT

This book is an outcome of the work done at the Institute for Social and Economic Change (ISEC), Bangalore, under the supervision and guidance of Dr. P. Hanumantha Rayappa, during the period 1979-84. Dr. Rayappa, in spite of his busy schedule always made it possible to find some time for guiding my work. His constant encouragement kept my spirit alive for the completion of this work. But for his guidance and encouragement, it would have been difficult for me to accomplish the task of producing this work. I am grateful to him.

I owe a debt of gratitude to Dr. N. Baskara Rao, Professor and Head, Population Research Centre, ISEC who patiently read through the type script of the work and made many constructive criticisms and valuable suggestions. I am indebted to Dr. Abdul Aziz, Professor and Head, Economics Unit, ISEC who gave generously of his time and counsel at many strategic points in the design and conduct of the investigation. Later on, he went through the type script and made many useful suggestions in order to bring out this work in the present shape.

Dr. P.M. Kulkarni, Associate Professor, Population Research Centre, ISEC who checked through the Methodology, especially the statistical techniques, and offered helpful comments made it possible to improve the quality of the exposition. Two other persons have been particularly helpful through the suggestions and criticisms they have given after reading the manuscript, Dr. C.S. Nagaraju, Associate Professor, ISEC especially in the parts dealing with education and Mr Deepak Grover, Assistant Professor, ISEC who took up himself an attempt to improve the language part of this work. My sincere thanks and appreciation are due to all of them.

Acknowledgement is due to Dr. M. Madaiah, Professor and Head, Department of Economics, University of Mysore who played a major role in initiating Demography as my area of interest when I was a student of that department during 1976-78.

Bulk of the literature that was necessary for this study was made available by the ISEC library. Remarkable co-operation was obtained from all the library staff in this venture. Literature pertaining to the topic was also made available by Ms Susan Pasquariella, Head Librarian, Centre for Population and Family Health, Columbia University, in response to my request. I would like to record my deep sense of gratitude to all of them. Thanks are also due to the organizations, *viz.* ILO, Population Council, CICRED and ESCAP for sending me relevant reading material on my request.

Acknowledgement is made for the role of ISEC in providing major financial support in the form of its fellowship for this work. In the final stages, financial support was rendered by Mr Ramesh Kanbargi, Director, Child Labour Project and Dr. Abdul Aziz, Director, Bidriware Project, through the Institute by way of providing me short-term employment.

Dr. Ram Deshpande, Assistant Professor, ISEC helped me out in using the computer for the data analysis. Ms. G. Rajamma who worked in different projects of the Institute extended her helping hand in the data processing stage.

Among my friends, who have read the manuscript in whole or in part and have made some suggestions, I would like to mention here the name of Mr B.C. Purohit, Ph.D. scholar, ISEC. I would like to express my appreciation and indebtedness to Ms. T. Sreedevi for her sympathetic support and encouragement during the long period involved in the preparation of this work. The person for whom I do not find any appropriate word to express my thanks is my friend Shirely Samuel but for whom this work would have been really an uphill task.

I wish to express my gratitude to Mr B.G. Kulkarni,

Assistant Professor, ISEC for his cartographical assistance. I must acknowledge my special indebtedness to Mr D. Nagaraj who did a prompt and an excellent work of typing the work. I am also grateful to Mr S.A. Prakash who so willingly did the work of duplicating the work.

Last but not least, the subjects of my study who live in the three villages of Dakshina Kannada district—Ajjavara, Mannur and Neriya—deserve my special thanks for their forbearance and co-operation extended to me during my stay in these villages.

B.M. Dinesh

CONTENTS

CONTENTS

LIST OF FIGURES

1

INTRODUCTION

1.1 Micro Theory of Fertility and Economic Benefits from Children

The micro theory of fertility distinguishes two kinds of parents' motives to have children, *viz.* the satisfaction they get by having children (psychic utility) and the prospective tangible returns that may accrue to them from their children (Schultz, 1971: Chapter 3; Schultz, 1973: 2; Willis, 1973: 16; Hoffman and Hoffman, 1973: 19-76; Arnold *et a l*, 1975; Simons, 1977: 157-180; Fawcett, 1978: 171-179). The latter motive constitutes the benefits that the parents expect from their children (a) as productive agents who contribute to the family income directly, (b) as substitutes for hired labour at home, on the family farm, in the family business or elsewhere, and (c) as a source of economic security to them when they are old and/or disabled. Leibenstein (1957: 48) calls these economic benefits from children as Income Utility, Work Utility and Security Utility, respectively. It has been argued that while the psychic utility motivates parents of urban families to have children, economic value of children is the major motivation of demand for children in the rural areas (Schultz, 1973: 5; Fawcett, 1972: 5-7; Caldwell, 1976b: 19; Wong, 1977: 323-324). This argument has been used by many demographers as an explanation for the rural-urban differentials in fertility.

Micro theory of fertility was first expounded by Becker (1960) with the help of Hicksian Indifference Curve Approach. His model was later criticized and modified by Blake (1968),

Mincer (1963: 75-79), Easterlin (1969), Namboodiri (1972), Leibenstein (1974 b), Caldwell (1976 a) and so on. While explaining the model Becker (1960) shows that the relationship between household income and the demand for children is positive, given the contraceptive knowledge and practice. "An increase in income increases both quantity and quality of children, but the quantity elasticity of demand for children is smaller than the quality elasticity of demand for children" (Becker, 1960: 174). Easterlin (1969) suggested a broader definition for the income concept used in Becker's model. He opined that the observed income at one point of time is not a true indicator of the income concept pertinent to a household's fertility decision and hence 'potential income flow through time' should be used. Observed income at one point of time inadequately reflects household's permanent income, for, it does not fully include household's prospective earnings at a point of time. The concept of 'potential income flow through time' measures both prospective income and the income foregone by the family at one point of time. In societies where children enter into labour force at early ages, the expectation of the contribution of children to family's prospective income would positively affect the fertility decisions of the parents. If the economic contribution of children is available to parents at a time when they are in family formation stage, then the tendency would be to produce more children with a view to increase the overall economic benefits accruing to parents from their children.

One of the important aspects in the micro theory of fertility on which discussion is centered is the concept of contraception. The pattern of differential fertility whereby the poor have more children and the rich have fewer, as Becker (1960) argues, can be explained with the help of the intervening variable namely, 'access to contraception'. Richer people are assumed to have greater access to contraception than the poor, which gives them more control over the supply of children. The contraceptive techniques were also assumed to be not widely known among the lower strata of the society. "If knowledge of contraceptive techniques did not vary with income, the relation between actual fertility and income would equal that between desired fertility and income" (Becker, 1960: 182). On the other hand Easterlin (1969) argued that no population is completely ignorant of contraceptive knowledge, for, contraceptive techniques like abstinence, withdrawal, abortion and infanticide have been universally known even in early times. It is, therefore, not the lack of contraceptive knowledge, but the pecuniary and psychological costs involved in the contraceptive practices which determine the differentials in fertility. It has been believed that in rural areas the psychological and monetary cost of contraceptive practices is more than the net cost of an additional child. The low net cost of children in these societies can be viewed as the outcome of the productive role of children from their youngest ages and a low pecuniary cost of bearing and rearing them. Many studies have shown that monetary cost of bearing and rearing farm children is much lower than that of non-farm children (Wong, 1977: 323-324). It has also been held that the opportunity cost of children in rural areas is quite smaller than that in urban areas (Ben-Porath, 1973: 202-233; Gronan, 1973: 200-201).

In order to explain the transition of societies from high fertility to low fertility Caldwell (1976 a) introduced a concept namely 'the inter-generational flow of wealth' (in the form of money, goods, services, guarantees and the like) in the micro theory. The crux of his argument is that in primitive and traditional societies the net flow of wealth (the flow from children to parents over the flow from parents to children) is unidirectional (from younger generation to older generation) during the period from when people become parents until they die. In these societies children have greater value to parents because they start contributing to parents' real income at very early ages, accept the responsibility for the care of parents in old age and when they are disabled and ensure the survival of the family name. These are considered as obligations of children and parents view them as the duties of their children.

In the context of the economic benefits that the parents obtain from their children, the time and resources used in bearing and rearing a child are considered in the micro-theory as investment costs towards the future productive capacity of the child. It is being argued that the investment motive for wanting children can be significant only in a situation where children begin to participate in economic activities at very early ages. In the developing countries where the cost of bearing and rearing children is low and where children enter into labour force at very early ages, a surviving child seems to be a good asset. Probably, this is the rationale of rural couples' preference for high fertility. However, it cannot be denied that the tangible contribution of children to household income has a major role to play in the fertility decision making of rural couples.

1.2 The Problem

High fertility and the resulting bottom heavy age structure are two important demographic characteristics of developing countries. In contrast to more developed countries developing nations have considerably larger proportions of population under fifteen years of age. For instance, in 1980, the world's less developed countries had about 39 per cent of their population under fifteen years of age, 57 per cent between ages fifteen and sixty-four years and 4 per cent in the age group of sixty-four plus. On the other hand, the more developed countries showed proportions in the same three age groups as 24 per cent, 65 per cent and 11 per cent, respectively (Population Reference Bureau, 1980). Nearly 41 per cent of population in India, 48 per cent in Liberia and 46 per cent in El Salvador is of children below fifteen years whereas among the rich countries 24 per cent population in Japan, 22 per cent in the USA and 23 per cent in the UK is under fifteen years of age. This contrasting feature of the developed and developing countries, with respect to the age structure, can be brought out more sharply by examining their child dependency ratios. The child dependency ratio in developing countries was about twice as high as that in developed countries. There were approximately four young dependents for every five persons in the working age group (15-64 years) in the developing countries as against the ratio of two young dependents to five persons (15-64 years) in the developed countries.

A young population has persisted in developing countries

throughout the period for which information is available (UN, 1973: 270). In recent decades the proportion of children in the total population has risen considerably in these countries. Of course, of late, there is a decline in child dependency. Out of an estimated child population of 1,500 million in the world in 1979, 81 per cent lived in less developed countries. Children of developing areas of Asia and Pacific region only, comprised 71 per cent of children of all developing countries and 57 per cent of the World's total child population (Population Reference Bureau, 1979).

A high birth rate, declining mortality rates and migration in a population, increases the child dependency ratio (UN, 1973: 270-281). In instances where fertility is high, there were correspondingly high proportions of young children in the 0-15 age group. This observation is reflected in the figures shown for the mean number of children ever born alive and proportion of population below 15 years presented for selected developed and developing countries of the world in Table 1.1. From the data presented in this Table, it is evident that child-dependency ratio is high in those countries where mean number of children born alive to a woman who has completed her reproductive life is high. The mean number of children born alive ranges between 4.8 and 6.3 in these countries. In developed countries the average number of children ever born, generally does not exceed three except in some Muslim and African countries like Turkey, Scychelles and Reunion. The family size is somewhat higher in these countries in spite of their high per capita income.

One of the important features common to most of the less developed countries is the prevalence of considerably low school enrolment ratios. In 1975, for example, the male and female school enrolment ratios for developing countries were 73 per cent and 53 per cent, respectively, in primary schools 42 per cent and 28 per cent respectively, in secondary schools as against 94 per cent for both the sexes in primary schools and 84 per cent and 85 per cent respectively in secondary schools for developed countries (Population Reference Bureau, 1979). Unlike developed nations, developing countries show significant sex differentials in school enrolment ratios in

TABLE 1.1: **Mean Number of Children, Per cent of Population Below Age 15 and the Child Dependency Ratio for Selected Developed and Developing Countries of the World**

Countries	*Mean number of children born alive for a woman of completed reproductive age (45-49)*	*Per cent of population below age 15*	*Child dependency ratio (%)*
Developed countries (per capita income $ 1,000+)			
1. Japan	2.78 (1970)	24	35.29
2. USA	2.85 (1970)	22	32.84
3. Argentina	2.88 (1970)	28	43.75
4. UK	2.02 (1961)	23	36.51
5. Australia	2.38 (1970)	27	42.19
Developing countries (per capita income below $ 1,000)			
1. Liberia	4.67 (1971)	48	96.00
2. Indonesia	4.83 (1963)	42	75.00
3. Thailand	6.32 (1970)	43	79.63
4. El-Salvador	6.33 (1971)	46	90.2[illegible]
5. India	Not available	41	73.21

Note: Figures in parentheses indicate the year for which data has been presented.

Sources:

1. United Nations, *Demographic Year Book*, 1973, Statistical Office, Department of Economics and Social Affairs, New York, 1974: 570-599.
2. United Nations, *Demographic Year Book*, 1971, Statistical Office, Department of Economics and Social Affairs, New York, 1972: 596-619.
3. United Nations, *Demographic Year Book*, 1969, Statistical Office, Department of Economics and Social Affairs, New York, 1970: 222-234.
4. Haub Carl and Heisler W. Douglas 1980, *World Population Data Sheet*, Population Reference Bureau, Washington DC.

favour of males as can be seen in Table 1.2. Data presented in this Table show that school enrolment ratios are either very low or fall very steeply as one progresses from primary schools to secondary schools in developing nations in comparison to the developed nations. Now the question is what do these children do who never went to school or who dropped out early? Available data indicate that a significant proportion of these children are engaged in work.

TABLE 1.2: **School Enrolment Ratios by Sex and Child Work Participation Rates for Selected Developed and Developing Countries of the World, 1975**

Country	*Primary school enrolment ratio (6-11 years of age)*		*Secondary school enrolment ratio (12-17 years of age)*		*Child work participation rate (5-14 years of age)*
	M	*F*	*M*	*F*	
Developed Countries (per capita income $ 1,000+)					
1. Japan	100	100	95	95	0.79
2. USA	99	99	95	96	0.87
3. Argentina	100	100	61	66	3.57
4. U.K.	98	98	85	85	0.01
5. Australia	99	99	82	80	0.57
Developing Countries (per capita income below $ 1,000)					
1. Liberia	45	29	59	24	8.49
2. Indonesia	66	58	42	32	6.78
3. Thailand	80	76	39	29	11.64
4. El-Salvador	62	63	56	49	5.75
5. India	73	49	36	19	9.49

Sources : 1. World Bank, *World Atlas of the Child*, World Bank Publication, 1979 : 36-39.

2. Cordell Mc Magda *et al*., *World Children Data Sheet*, Population Reference Bureau, Washington DC, 1979.

Several attempts have been made to estimate the magnitude of working children, in the world, on the basis of data collected from censuses and other sources. According to the 1979 ILO Statistics there were about 52 million working children in the world accounting for 1.2 per cent of the total population. Out of the estimated 52 million working children 95 per cent were found in less developed countries. Highest work participation rates for children were found in African countries followed by South East Asian, East Asian and Latin American countries. Among the South East Asian countries, India alone has nearly one-eighth of the total child labour of the world.

Based on work participation and schooling, children can be classified into four categories, *viz.* (a) those who go to school but do not work; (b) those who work but do not go to school; (c) those who go to school as well as work; and (d) those who neither go to school nor work. The quantification of all these categories of children requires cross-classification of census data for child work participation and non-participation against attendance or enrolment in schools. But such classifications are seldom made in census tabulations (United Nations, 1968:57). In the 1971 Census of India, data are provided for children whose main activities are reported as 'working', 'studying' and 'neither working nor studying'. The last category is further split into (a) those who are performing household duties, (b) dependents, (c) infants, rentiers and persons of independent means, (d) beggars, vagrants, etc. (e) inmates of penal, mental and charitable institutions and (f) others who are not engaged in any activity but are seeking work. Thus the classification of children according to main activity overlooks one important class of children, *viz.* those who combine schooling and work. This seems to be a very significant proportion. In rural Chile, for example, about 66 per cent of children aged nine to fifteen were attending school full-time, another 12 per cent were engaged in full-time work activities and nearly 22 per cent were combining schooling and work (Rodgers and Standing, 1981: 35).

In addition to children who combine work with schooling, other categories of children may also be performing work as a secondary or marginal activity. Also working children and school-going children may be devoting some time to perform household duties. But data on such details are lacking in many of the developing countries, especially in India. Hence the need to collect information on the complete activity profile of children in less developed countries is suggested, to study the economic activities they perform and to assess the level of their participation. To accomplish this Rodger and Standing (1981) distinguished nine possible categories of time use by children. These are:

1. domestic work which is performed by children in almost all kinds of societies;
2. non-domestic, non-monetary work which are familial productive activities;
3. bonded labour to pay off debts;
4. wage labour;
5. marginal economic activities which is a set of activities in the informal sector including both legitimate and illegitimate activities;
6. schooling;
7. unemployment;
8. recreation or leisure which is different from idleness due to unemployment by its voluntary nature, and
9. activities such as sleeping, eating, washing and related personal care.

Information regarding time allocation by children to these activities is important because it helps to measure the direct and indirect, and formal and informal economic contribution of children to their household economies. According to micro-theory of fertility these economic contribution of children have a significant bearing on fertility in less developed areas.

Past research on fertility has taken into account the role of children as an element in fertility decision making of couples (Schultz, 1970: 10-49; Harman, 1970: 3-47; Davanzo, 1972: 36-40, 84-87; De Tray, 1972: 19-24; Rosenzweig and Evenson, 1977: 1065-1079). Some of the studies on economic activities of children have shown that child labour significantly contributes to the household economy (These studies have been reviewed in the following chapter). But in the specific setting of India, only a few fragmentary pieces of evidence are available on this topic. Hence the present study has been planned to focus on the economic activities of children in the Indian context in a greater detail.

1.3 Objectives of the Present Study

The present study enquires into the dimensions, causes and consequences of the participation of children in economic activities in rural areas. The overall objective of the study is, of course, to assess the economic contribution of children to the household economy in rural areas. The specific objectives, however, are:

1. To study the participation of children in economic activities at home and outside home in terms of:
   - (a) the magnitude of work;
   - (b) the intensity of work;
   - (c) the place of work;
   - (d) the nature of activities performed, and
   - (e) the wages earned.
2. To study the compatibility and/or competitiveness of work and schooling of children in rural situations.
3. To identify the causes of child work participation in rural areas.
4. To highlight some of the consequences of child work participation.
5. To understand parents' perceptions of the importance of economic contribution of children.

1.4 Outline of the Study

Besides the present chapter, this study contains eight more chapters. The following chapter presents a review of related studies on the topic. Chapter-3 gives a logical elaboration on the hypothesized causes and consequences of the participation of children in economic activities. Chapter-4 concentrates on analysing available data on child work participation. In

Chapter-5, the need for a primary investigation and the methodology are given.

The interpretation of the results of the primary investigation is presented in Chapter-6, 7 and 8. Chapter-6 deals with the dimensions of the economic activities of children and Chapter-7 with its causes and consequences. Chapter-8 illustrates parents' perceptions of the work and security utility of children. The summary of the findings of the study and their implications are given in Chapter-9.

2

A REVIEW OF RELATED LITERATURE

To get a better insight into the problem, a brief review of the available studies on 'economic activities of children' is presented. This review includes a few related studies carried out abroad and a few fragmentary pieces of information available from studies carried out in India. The review focuses on the findings of these studies with regard to the dimensions, causes and consequences of child work participation. The review is intended to identify research gaps on the topic which would help us to raise some issues for detailed discussion in the study.

2.1 Economic Contribution of Children

A major attempt to collect valuable data on work-input of children in peasant societies was that of Nag, White and Peet (1978: 293-306). Their study conducted in two backward communities of Java (Indonesia) and Nepal found that in both the villages economic contribution of children to the household was quite substantial. The economic contribution was measured by them in terms of the average time spent in each activity by both male and female children. In a similar study undertaken in a village—Char Gopalpur—in Bangladesh, Cain (1977: 201-229) found that children of both the sexes put in considerably long hours of work. According to him a high fertility and a large number of surviving children are economically a rational proposition for the rural couples of Bangladesh due to their significant contribution to the household income. Caldwell's study in Nigeria (1977: 5-27) attempted to measure and analyse the activities of children by sex, age, education and so on. Data collected by him showed that children perform variety of tasks as early as five years of age. In Philippines, Madigan (1977: 278) noticed children of even less than five years of age carrying messages and making small purchases. In Thailand, Buripkadi (1977: 109-110) observed a negative association between the expected economic help from children and both birth control attitudes of parents and the current use of birth control. He attributes this finding to the economic value attached to child labour by parents. Peek (1978: 177-190) in an analysis of the survey data collected from two cities of the Third World tried to show to what extent the contribution of children to household income is determined by socio-economic factors. From the findings of his analysis, he concludes that the fertility levels are determined by the value of children but the economic value itself is determined by the socio-economic variables.

Similar observations, though not in detail, have been made in the Indian context. A significant one among them was that of Mamdani (1972). He explains why the poor households in the village Manipur desire to have large families and as such do not accept family planning. The evidence presented by him corroborates his argument that children perform variety of activities which are directly or indirectly beneficial to parents. A similar view is held by Nadkarni (1976: 1163-1172). His socio-economic survey conducted on a census basis in six villages of Maharashtra State showed high child work participation rates among the small land owners and agricultural labourers. In another survey, conducted to study the economic rationality of family reproduction of a fishing community in Vizakapattnam, Murthy and Rao (1979: 253-272) observed a large proportion of children employed productively. They also observed the fertility rate of this community tending to be high.

Contradicting the findings of the above mentioned researches, Vlassoff's study in a village in Maharashtra state of India (1979: 415-428) showed low work participation rates for adolescent boys below age sixteen and very low rates for younger children. Contrasting observations of Vlassoff's study and other similar studies may be due to the definitional differences especially on 'work'. Nevertheless it is presumable that definitional variations make up a large part of the differences in work participation.

Mueller (1976: 98-153) made an attempt to estimate the actual net economic value of children in less developed countries. She examined the economic value of children at two levels, *viz.* at macro level to the society at large and at micro level to parents in the agricultural sector. She constructed scales of relative consumption and production to gauge their levels for different age groups of the population and the society. The consumption profile was measured in relation to the amount of adult consumption per unit of time taken as one consumption unit. The production profile, on the other hand, was the average work contribution of each age-sex group in relation to that of adult males. Analysis of the consumption and production profiles of society as a whole revealed that children have a net economic cost or a negative economic value by consuming more than what they produce. In case of an individual couple, Mueller estimated the difference between production and consumption over their life span. Families with two, four and six children were studied. Assuming standard and higher production and medium consumption, it was found that the potential saving rate was higher for the couple with two children, medium for the couple with four children and lower for the couple with six children. In other words, larger the number of children, smaller the potential savings and *vice-versa.* Having too many children, therefore, according to her, is an economic loss for an individual parent over their life cycle.

Using age-wise data from Bangladesh on average daily per person calorie consumption requirements for children, Cain (1977: 201-229) found out the age at which a child becomes a net producer and the age at which a child produces an amount equal to his total consumption up to that point. Contrary to Mueller's findings his analysis showed that after ten years of age the male children become net producers and after age fifteen, their cumulative production exceeds their cumulative consumption. He concluded that landless parents enjoy a net economic return from their male children even when they are subordinate members of the parental households. Assuming zero contribution from female children, a male child is calculated to produce for his cumulative consumption and for that of one sister by age twenty-two if she gets married at age fifteen. The findings of Mueller and Cain differ in regard to the net economic benefits of children to parents. Nevertheless, there is a common point as far as the economic activities of children are concerned. Both Mueller and Cain agree that children do contribute to the household income.

For Bangladesh, Cain made observations regarding children's time inputs to work. He found that by age four to six they work approximately o e-fifth of an adult working day, by age seven to nine one-half nd by age ten to twelve they work three quarters as long as adults. Children aged thirteen and above were found working on an average as long as or longer than adults. Hull (1977: 242) in his summary of the two studies (Hull, 1975; Nag *et al.*, 1977) states that the intensity of child work participation increases with increase in age and it reaches adult level by adolescence. A similar trend is noticed in Thailand as well (Suchart, 1977: 311). Age-wise variations in the intensity of work is caused by the variations in the intensity of participation in directly productive activities rather than in household activities (Nag, White and Peet, 1978: 294). Vlassoff 1979: 422) also noticed age-wise variations in the work-inputs of children, but data presented by him showed comparatively lower intensity of work among children of both the sexes. Boys were found working, on an average, not more that 2.1 hours per day before they cross age fifteen and girls not more than 0.5 hours before twelve years of age.

Sex differentials in child work participation is another aspect highlighted in many of the studies on the topic. In Nigeria, Caldwell noticed sex differentials in the activities performed by children (1977: 22). But data presented by Cain do not show significant sex differentials in the overall work input of children (1977: 216). In Java and Nepal Nag *et al.*, observed sex differentials in the activities performed by children. The sex-wise work-input tables presented by them for these villages show the work-inputs to be in favour of girls than boys (1978: 294-296). Even in the case of directly productive activities, girls of nine years and above were found to be spending more time than boys of the same age-group. In Thailand, higher work participation rate is found in household duties than in occupational work (non-household) and higher intensity of work is noticed for girls than for boys (Suchart, 1977: 311). Information elicited by Vlassoff from the adult men about the contribution their children made to the household income also shows higher participation rates and higher intensity of work by daughters than by sons (1979: 421-422). Nadkarni's study gave us similar results in this regard (1976: 1169).

The low intensity of work participation of boys in comparison to girls may be due to the sex-selectivity in getting certain activities performed. For instance, in certain societies household duties and other allied activities are allowed to be performed only by girls whereas boys are engaged in comparatively tougher tasks. Since household duties are daily chores and involve more time, the work-input of girls is generally higher than that of boys. Parents extract as much works as possible from their daughters in the process of training them into full-time house-wives before they are given in marriage.

2.2 Child Work Participation and the Opportunity Cost of Women's Participation in Labour Force

It has been believed by some economists and demographers that in poor families children engaged in domestic chores free women for seeking productive employment outside home. Hull (1977: 244), for example, observed a steep decline in the intensity of parents' participation in household duties over their life cycle as their children grew older. Alongside he noticed increased participation of women in economic activities outside home after the early years of their marriage. Snyders' econometric analysis (1974: 622) of the Sierra Leon data for family size and mothers' time for market work showed positive relationship. He suggested that this may be because wives find it necessary to work to support a large family and/or they find it easier to work because elder children can perform some of the household work. In Caldwell's survey, ninety per cent of his respondents agree that children are important since they save adults from menial tasks (1977: 22). Nadkarni presented data to show that a large proportion of children are retained for household work among the small land-owners and agricultural labourers (1976: 1171). In Ghana, Oppong (1973: 51) found their services indispensable to their parents, for, by carrying out some time-consuming activities they not only give parents time to do more productive activities but also fetch them enough leisure. Mamdani (1972: 99) showed with illustrations how a farmer's wife over-burdened with domestic chores was relieved of her 'intolerable hardship' by having more children. However, none of these studies made any attempt to measure the extent to which children can or do substitute for their parents. If children allow parents free to do more productive work outside home the intensity of children's participation in such activities will determine the opportunity cost of parents' work outside home.

2.3 Sibling Number as Determining Factor of Child Work Participation

Yet another aspect which Nag, White and Peet (1978: 297) highlighted in their work is the effect of number of siblings on the work-input of children. Contrary to the general belief that work-input of children in smaller families is more than that in large families, they found children in larger families tending to be more productive (in terms of time-input) than those in smaller families. They presume that this may be because,

1. younger children in large families are encouraged by the example of elder siblings to participate in all kinds of work at an early age and/or
2. the elder children of larger families are free to engage in directly productive activities as their younger sibling do the household chores.

Whatever may be the reason, the data presented by Nag *et al.*, indicate that in both Java and Nepal children devote a significant part of their work time in taking care of younger siblings. Obviously, in larger families elder children will be having more number of younger siblings to take care of than in smaller families. Anyway, the reasons suspected by Nag *et al.*, in this respect can be tested by asking direct questions and by tabulating the work-input of older children in various activities by the number of younger siblings they have.

2.4 Land Ownership and Child Work Participation

Another aspect which has been touched upon by many of the studies mentioned above is the association of child labour with the size of land holding. In Java, White observed a negative relation between size of land holding and the economic contribution of children. According to him, the more closely the household approaches landlessness, the more is the work performed by both adults and children (Nag, 1972b: 305). A more or less similar trend was found by Shortlidge (1976) in Uttar Pradesh. His findings indicated that boys under age fifteen in households with over fifteen acres of land did not work on the farm at all, whereas 45 to 49 per cent of boys, aged between eleven and fifteen of agricultural labour households and small cultivator households were found working. Data has been provided by Nadkarni to show the differentials in work participation of children between different cultivator groups classified according to the size of their operational holdings. Data presented by him indicated the highest child work participation among the very poor class (cultivators with less than 5 acres, agricultural labourers and others), moderately high among the moderately poor class (cultivators with 5-10 acres and artisans) and lowest among the non-poor class (cultivators with more than 10 acres) (Nadkarni, 1976: 1165). Thus the observed association between the size of land holding and child labour in Java also holds good for the Marathwada region of Maharashtra. Vlassoff, on the contrary, did not find the same relationship for a village in Maharashtra. He reported that children were economically active only among rich families and argues that the rich families who owned more land also provide more opportunities for the economic contribution of their children (1979: 424).

An attempt was made by Cain also to indicate the affect of the size of land-holding on child labour. His sample of households was divided into three economic classes based on the size of land-holding, *viz.* (1) large land owners, (2) small land owners, and (3) landless. Data collected for the economic activities of children from these three classes of households showed that below age ten, boys from landless households work less than boys from landed households (Cain, 1977: 217). Productivity-wise boys of well-to-do families were found to be engaged in more productive activities than the boys of landless families. He finds these observations consistent with the unequal control of productive assets by these classes of people.

The available evidence on the incidence of child work participation in households with different size of land holding or income classes is not uniform. The ownership of assets including land may promote child work participation or deter it. The relation observed with respect to economic position of the household and child work participation may not be unidirectional up to some threshold level. The negative relationship between these two variables may operate only after a certain break-even point.

2.5 Caste and Child Work Participation

The relationship between caste and child work participation is another dimension to be studied in the Indian context. But, no empirical evidence is available on this aspect. Rayappa and Grover, however, have provided data from twelve villages of Tamil Nadu State to show higher work participation rates among children (5-14) belonging to Scheduled Castes and Scheduled Tribes than among children belonging to non-Scheduled groups (1980: 53).

2.6 Seasonal Variation in the Work-Input of Children

Nadkarni detected considerable seasonal variation in the work-input of children in rural Maharashtra. According to him busy seasons in villages are marked by labour shortages with reciprocally greater absenteeism in village schools (1976: 1171). In Nigeria, Okore (1977: 263-264) noticed that Ibos of Imo State realised the importance of child labour during the peak farming period. He found them employing young children from the age of seven onwards to transport the yarns from the barn to the farm land for planting and from the farm back to the barn during harvesting. Mamdani, on the other hand, opines that seasonality in child labour does not exist because children are mostly engaged in either looking after cattle or performing house-work (1972: 100). This view contradicts Mellor's hypothesis which holds that seasonal equilibrium between demand for and supply of labour is struck by the introduction and withdrawal of children and women in the labour market (1976: 90-95). Even if children are engaged exclusively in household chores, they may put in more work during busy season by working more at home so as to enable their parents to perform their additional farm work during peak seasons. According to Mellor's hypothesis labour scarcity is the cause for seasonal variations in child labour in farming societies. Labour scarcity may be due to certain time consuming tasks or overall peak labour demand created during busy seasons which results in children to enter the labour market. Prevailing low wage rates for children for the same quantity of certain work activities done by adults induce employers to employ children for performing such types of activities during busy seasons.

2.7 Irrigational Facility as an Encouraging Factor for Child Work Participation

Irrigation leads to overall higher labour requirements and thus facilitates the participation of children in work. The Bench Mark Survey conducted in the drought-prone areas commanded by Malaprabha and Ghataprabha projects of Karnataka State showed that among both sexes the percentage of children working in irrigated settlements was much higher than the percentage of children working in settlements which were yet to be irrigated. The participation rate of children in work was higher in the rainfed settlements lying outside the command area than in the command area itself (Srikantan, *et al.*, 1978: 10).

2.8 Perceptions of the Importance of Child Labour

Besides measuring the economic contribution of children in developing societies, some of the studies have made attempts to elicit information about parents' perceptions of the importance of child labour. In rural Maharashtra, Vlassoff tried to assess the value parents attached to child labour. He asked parents to categorise the economic contribution of their children as perceived by them into the following categories, viz. (1) of much help, (2) of some help, and (3) of no help. Their responses to his queries strongly suggested that the majority of parents did not regard child labour as an important economic contribution. Mueller's study (1972: 383-403) in Taiwan showed that only a few Taiwanese husbands regard the work-input of children as economically advantageous. In contrast, in Manupur, Mamdani (1972: 144) noticed parents attaching great value to the working children as a source of family income. Questions were also asked by Murthy and Rao (1979: 253-272) to know parents' perceptions of the economic advantage of children. Answers thus collected showed that 60 per cent of the respondents perceived a large number of children as economically beneficial and for onl 30 per cent, they were not advantageous. The Value Of Children Project (VOC) in its comparative study of three socio-economic classes, *viz.* upper middle, lower middle and rural poor, arrived at a similar conclusion (Fawcet, *et al.*, 1974). Of late, Zachariah's study of Kerala and Karnataka states of India also showed that parents perceive children as the main source of financial support in old age (Zachariah and Newlon, 1983: 240).

2.9 Research Gaps and Issues

The foregoing review discusses the findings of related studies on dimensions of child work participation such as the work participation rates, work intensity, place of work, nature of activities performed, age at which they start performing various activities, sex differentials in their economic contribution, etc. determinants of child work participation such as land-ownership, sibling number, caste, etc. and the consequence of child work participation in terms of their work contribution to the household economy which brings down the opportunity cost of women's participation in labour force. The review, however, brings to our cognizance two major research gaps in this area which need to be given due attention. These are:

1. information regarding the compatibility and competitiveness of work and schooling of children are lacking in the previous studies. Children in the population by work-school status is, thus, a major data gap. Analysis of data on child work participation by schooling status has an implication on the magnitude of work, intensity of work, nature of activities performed and wages earned. In other words, it has an implication on the impact of overall economic contribution of children or child schooling and non-schooling, and
2. comprehensive information regarding the socio-economic and demographic determinants (causes) of child work participation are lacking, especially in the Indian context.

The above mentioned research gaps raise certain issues to be pursued for a thorough discussion. These are:

(i) do children combine schooling and work? If so, do they form a significant proportion?
(ii) if a significant proportion of children are combining schooling and work, do the magnitude, intensity and the nature of work performed by them and the wages earned or their tangible contribution vary significantly from those who work without going to school? and
(iii) what are the factors which determine child work participation and its consequences?

The discussion in the present study is centred around these issues.

3

HYPOTHESIZED CAUSES AND CONSEQUENCES OF CHILDREN'S PARTICIPATION IN ECONOMIC ACTIVITIES

Several factors are expected to be the causes of the participation of children in economic activities. These are poverty, caste, tradition, size of the family, labour scarcity, wage rates, illiteracy, schooling facilities, neighbourhood effect, etc. These factors are interlinked and exert their influence directly and/or indirectly on the work participation of children. The hypothesized influences of these factors on child work participation is diagrammatically represented in Fig. 3.1. Fig. 3.2 shows the possible consequences of child work participation on the child, on the family and on the society. This chapter presents a logical elaboration on the various causes and consequences of children's participation in economic activities.

3.1 Causes

Poverty: Poverty is a common feature of developing countries. In these countries, a considerable proportion of the population lives below the poverty line. The term poverty line refers to a line "drawn in the light of the socially expected minimum standard of living" (Sen, 1974: 67-68). All those persons whose standard of living is below this minimum are called 'absolute poor'. In developing countries a large proportion of the poor is found in the rural areas. They are mostly concentrated in the agricultural sector. In India, for

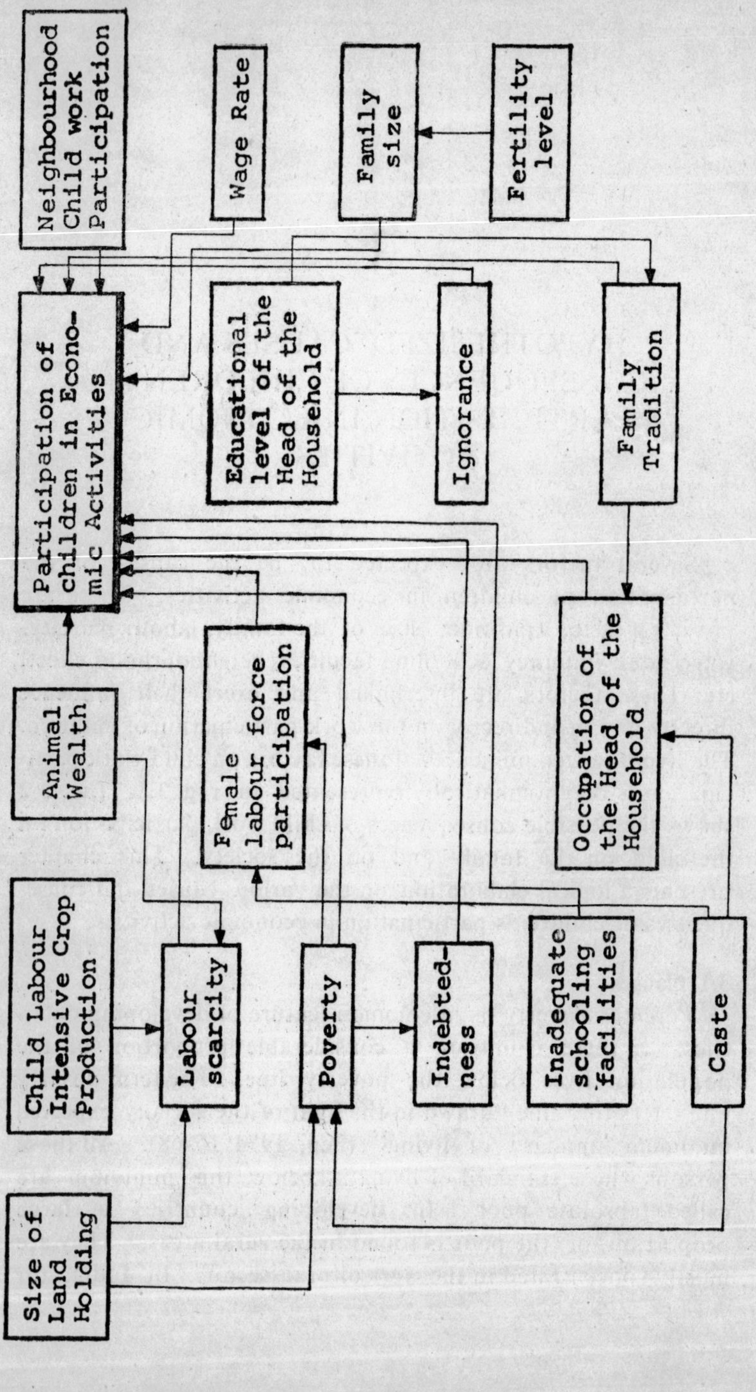

Fig. 3.1 : Causes of Child Work Participation : A Schematic Representation.

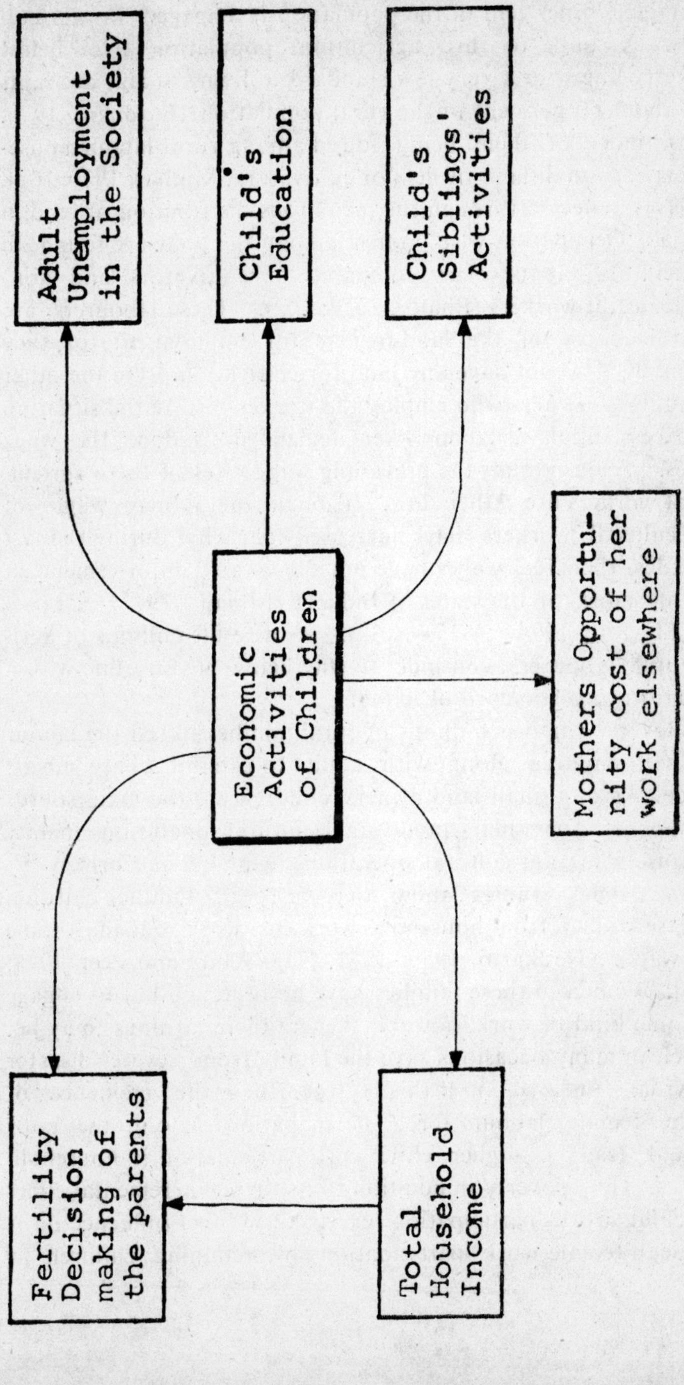

Fig. 3.2 : Consequences of Child Work Participation : A Schematic Representation

example, 70 per cent of the population is engaged in agriculture. A bulk of this agricultural population lives below poverty line with a very low standard of living. This accounts for about 60 per cent of the rural population (Bardhan, 1970: 135), most of them being found among rural labour households and small land owners or cultivators (Minhas, 1970: 107). This is reflected through the inequitous distribution of land in India. Occupation-wise poorest among the poor are found in agricultural labour class compared to cultivators and non-agricultural workers (Bhatty, 1974: 302). These labourers are at the mercy of the land-owners for employment, for, they themselves do not have any land for cultivation. On the other hand, land-owners who employ the workers utilize the situation of excess supply of labour over demand to reduce the wage rates. As a result the prevailing wage rates of these agricultural workers are rather low. Though the money wages of agricultural workers have increased somewhat during the last decades, their real wages have not shown any improvement at all in most of the states of India (Krishnaji, 1971: A 148—A 151; Jose, 1974: A 25—A 30). As a result millions of agricultural labourers continue to stay below poverty line with a deteriorating standard of living.

Poverty compels millions of rural families to sell the labour of their children along with adults to eke out a bare subsistence. Among small land owners, children are the main source of support for their family agricultural operations mainly because some agricultural operations can be performed by them. Some studies show that in poor families children release women from household work to work outside home for wages (Nadkarni, 1976: 1171; Nag, White and Peet, 1978: 297). Women in these families have no other go but to engage in some kind of work, however meagre their earnings may be, which in many occasions save the family from severe disaster (Myrdal, 1968: 1073). If this is true, then the incidence of higher female labour force participation among the poor should lead to higher child work participation in household duties. Thus poverty in addition to its direct incremental effect on child work participation exerts an indirect influence on it through female work participation by retaining children at home and engaging them in household and family activities.

Poverty leads to indebtedness. Adult members of indebted households can neither save to clear off their debts nor can they leave their existing activities and work under the creditor to pay them off, for, their present earnings are essential for family survival. In such a situation they send their children to work under the creditor to clear off their debts. In some cases this takes the form of bonded labour perpetuated into life long bondage. Poverty and child labour, thus, go hand in hand and tend to reinforce each other in poor families and communities.

Poverty leads to illiteracy. In majority of the cases it is the inability of parents to spare some money which keeps their children away from school. To satisfy the immediate vital needs, parents have to forego satisfying some or all of their children's needs with respect to education and recreation. A large proportion of those who do not go to school are generally sent to work. Children who are thus denied the benefits and opportunities of education become illiterate parents when they grow up.

Caste: Caste system is one of the several forms of stratification of the Society (Harper, 1970: 51). It is "a class of the community which disowns any connection with any other class and can neither inter-marry nor eat or drink with any but persons of their own community". It has "a collection of families or groups of families bearing a common name which usually denotes or is associated with specific occupation claiming common descent from a mythical ancestor, human or divine, professing to follow the same professional callings and are regarded by those who are competent to give an opinion as forming a single homogeneous community" (Ketkar, 1979: 4). Its membership is limited only to those who are born within the group (Ketkar, 1979: 15). In recent years, however, inter-caste marriage and inter-occupational mobility are more common, but still exceptions rather than rule.

The economic structure of the society is influenced by the caste factor. The rural rich is usually found among the upper castes and the poor among the lower castes. A study conducted by the Institute for Public Opinion in 1969 shows that 41 per cent of the population in India is below the poverty line, out of which about one-half belongs to the Scheduled Castes and Scheduled Tribes (as cited by Kulshrestha, 1978: 13). In villages a vast majority of agricultural labourers belong to these communities and hence a majority of child labour must also be found among them.

It is generally found that women work participation rates are high among those sections of the people who rank low in the caste hierarchy (Arles, 1971: 29-64; Myrdal, 1968: 1073). So there seems to be a close relationship between women work participation and the caste factor. The influence of caste on women work participation can be explained in two ways. First, there is a social status consciousness attached to the women of upper castes which makes them reluctant to participate in work activities outside home. But the lower caste women do not have any such social status consciousness and hence take up jobs when need arises. Moreover, activities generally taken up by the lower castes do not require any formal education or training and therefore are easier for them to perform (Radhadevi, 1978: 32).

The influence of women work participation on the work participation of children has already been discussed. We concluded that child work participation is high in those families where women labour force participation is high, for, children are retained at home to perform household and other allied activities to free the women to participate in work force.

Tradition: It has been observed that even in situations where there is no compelling necessity, a child is traditionally expected to contribute to the family income (Mendelvich, 1979: 560). This is because parents traditionally perceive certain advantages in child work participation. They believe that the child will be disciplined by entering labour force, it is prestigious to the family if the child terminates its dependency at the earliest age, child is protected against delinquent culture by taking up a job, it provides their parents moments of privacy, in cases of parental incapacitation early in life they can depend on children if they start working early in life and so on. "Children too, in many cases, have the fear of being discarded by their parents if they do not earn and prove they are useful to the family" (Government of India, 1979: 11).

In India, tradition does not favour sending girls to school. This may be one of the reasons why duration of schooling is briefer for girls compared to boys. Girls are traditionally expected to learn and perform domestic chores because these are essential training for future house-wives and education is regarded as irrelevant for that task. Even if girls enter primary schools, ". . . after the first year of school, custom and the need to keep girls at home to help in the house work, and look after the younger children and in some areas early marriage, resulted in considerable wastage among girl pupils" (Myrdal, 1968: 1726).

Family Size: Fertility performance of a woman depends upon many factors like age at marriage, infant mortality, sex composition of surviving children, economic status of the family, religion and so on. Given the infant mortality a high fertility leads to a large family size. The relationship between family size and child work participation is assumed to be direct among poor families. In large families of the lower strata of the society parents are forced to send some of their children to work, for, the available resources do not allow them to send all their children to school. Only a few children (generally male) of these families attend school and others work either to support the expenses of their school going siblings or to keep away from idleness.

Labour Scarcity: Agricultural activities are characterised by two seasons, *viz.* busy season and off season. During busy season, there is labour scarcity in the agricultural labour market because the demand for labour is more than its supply. During off season, the extra labour is thrown out of production (Myrdal, 1968: 1075-1076) Thus, seasonality in agriculture causes seasonal disequilibrium between demand for and supply of labour in the agricultural labour market. The equilibrium is restored by the introduction and withdrawal of children and women in the labour market (Mellor, 1976: 95). Accordingly, seasonal variations in child labour are the result of labour scarcity during busy season. During these seasons certain time consuming, less productive but important activities like weeding, guarding crops, etc. are created for which the supply of adult labour is scarce. In such a situation the employer entertains children to work and the poor households, in an effort to restore the economic balance of the family, send their children to work for small pittance. As in agriculture, seasonal variations in employment are found in certain non-agricultural activities also. The same mechanism operates in the introduction and withdrawal of children in the non-agricultural activities as well.

The cultivators, sometimes, have to hire-in labour for cultivation. A large cultivator, generally a rich cultivator, can afford to do so. Small and marginal cultivators who are cultivating for their subsistence and in several cases highly indebted, have no other go but to send their children to work on their family farm or to retain them at home to release women to work on the farm

In agriculture, the incidence of child work participation varies with the cropping pattern. If the cropping pattern is such that a larger proportion of crops grown are child labour intensive, obviously the incidence of child work participation in that area is high. Raising of crops which involves more time-consuming and unskilled activities provide more opportunities for children to enter into labour force. Crops grown like jowar, cotton, groundnut, etc. require less skill during harvesting and they involve time consuming activities such as picking, sorting and cleaning. Crops like paddy, wheat, ragi, etc. on the other hand, require more skilled work and hence are not child labour intensive.

When irrigational facilities are available to the cultivator throughout the year, the seasonality in agriculture is minimised by increasing the number of busy seasons and reducing the span of slack seasons. As a result, there will be a persisting demand for child labour due to the creation of child labour intensive activities which may lead to higher child work participation rates in those areas (Myrdal, 1968: 1077-1078).

The possession of live-stock such as cattle, sheep, etc. by a family also demands children to work. The work involved in caring for and tending these animals are so time consuming that children's services are often sought. The elder members of the family engage in other more productive activities which fetch them direct returns and for which hard labour is necessary.

Wage Rates: The relation between wage rate and economic activities of children is direct. An increase in wage rate for children normally increases the child work participation rates in the initial stages. When the demand for labour is in excess of the supply, the wage rate is increased. Given the full employment of the available child labour in a given area, the creation of additional activities for which only children are preferred or adult labour is scarce leads to an increase in child wage rates to attract more children from school to work and to pirate more workers from other employers.

Schooling Facilities: In developing countries, a significant proportion of children are denied of their education due to the inadequacy and the inaccessibility of schooling facilities. By the standards of Western countries, in these nations the conventional minimum age of entry into the potential labour force is low because of the absence of comprehensive, compulsory and adequate-accessible educational facilities. In India, for example, out of about 548,000 villages as many as 50,000 villages were without schools and more than 160,000 rural schools were functioning with only one teacher a piece. "In most places, the school presents a drab and dismal picture and holds little attraction for the child" (Government of India, 1979: 12).

Absence of educational facilities in a village deprives children of their opportunities of education. Children have to travel long distance to neighbouring villages for attending schools, if schooling facilities are not available in their home villages. Parents who are willing to send their children to schools find schooling of children more expensive when it involves travelling expenses. Some of them feel it risky to send their children to neighbouring villages for attending school (particularly female children) as children have to leave home early in the morning and can come back only late in the evening. As a result, many parents are reluctant to enrol their children in schools. Even if they are enrolled, the inconveniences experienced by children make them dropout early from schools. Thus children who do not go to school have two alternatives—they either remain idle without doing any work or participate in economic activities. As parents of these children would like them to do some kind of work instead of remaining idle, they are thus compelled to engage in economic activities.

Neighbourhood Effect: "The neighbourhood is ordinarily viewed as a smaller version of a local community" [Sills (ed.), 1972: 121]. It is ". . . a group of people experiencing social interaction within a localised area with one or two social Institutions as the focal point or means by which the area can be identified physically" [Bertrand (ed.), 1958: 77].

Neighbourhood households have some social ties. They participate in one another's family rituals, help one another by lending utensils, food or by exchanging labour and more than all, they discuss on family matters like family health, occupation, children's education, etc. on a common platform. Men gather in verandhas or workshops during leisure time whereas women make use of their trips to those places where women of neighbouring households meet (Mandelbaun, 1972: 341). This type of get-togethers of neighbours are of great importance as their attitudes and behaviour influence the attitudes and behaviour of a family. If neighbouring households send their children to work, that might positively influence the attitudes of the parents towards child labour. On the contrary if the neighbouring households send their children to schools, that might induce a parent to send his children also to school. This is termed as neighbourhood effect.

A locality is usually determined by the factors like caste and income. Neighbours of an upper caste household are normally found to be belonging to upper caste and that of a lower caste household belonging to lower caste. Admittedly, the attitudes of these groups towards engaging children in work is predetermined by other factors. However, by neighbourhood effect we mean the influence of neighbourhood households alone on the economic activities of children of a family within the group.

3.2 Consequences

The first and foremost consequence of the participation of children in economic activities is on their own health and education. The work participation of children adversely affects their health and education, partially or fully, depending upon the degree of their participation in work. There are two categories of child workers—one which consists of those who do not go to school at all and the other category consists of those who work as well as go to school. Children of the first category remain illiterate in their life. Children who are in the second category could hardly attend classes regularly due to their involvement in work activities and as a result they dropout gradually due to repetitions and slow progress. Consequently these children fail to reap the fruits of education fully even though they are literate by definition. "The lack of literacy is equivalent to the lack of nutrition in early child development which causes fatal damage or retardation in brain development and physical growth" (Correa, 1979: 77). Early participation in hazardous activities shortens their length of life and their future earnings. As Woodward puts it (Kulshrestha, 1978: 10) for every dollar earned by a child under fourteen years of age ten fold will be taken from its earning capacity in later years".

Child work participation contributes to the household income directly and/or indirectly. Children's work at home, on the family farm and in the family business are their intangible contributions to the household income, whereas when they work outside the family enterprise, for returns in cash and/or kind they could supplement their family income in real terms.

Children help their family also by reducing the opportunity cost of their mothers' work outside home. The opportunity cost of mothers' work outside home is nothing but the activities and income mothers sacrifice at home to perform their work outside home. It has already been mentioned that children free women (especially mothers) from household chores to enable them to participate in labour force. The extent to which they free women refers to the consequence of their work activities.

Economic activities of children add to their economic value to parents in rural societies. They regard them as productive agents and hence as assets to the family. The more the number of children a family has got, the stronger it becomes financially is the norm they stick on to. A rural family, therefore, would prefer to have many children, expecting each one of them to work and add to the family income. High fertility, hence, is one of the consequences of the economic activities of children.

Employers view the employment of children as advantageous. As child labour is paid less than adult labour, it emerges as a source of cheap labour for the employer. Besides, children have less developed ego and status consciousness and are less afflicted by feelings of guilt and shame. A consequence of the employment of children on the community is that it reduces adult wages. All the more it displaces adults from the labour market and adds to the unemployment problem. It has been estimated that atleast fifteen million vacancies can be created for the adult unemployed by siphoning off the existing child labour in India (as cited in Kulshrestha, 1978: 9).

Finally, the work participation of children encourages their siblings also to participate in labour force. Many a time children imitate their elder brothers and sisters which eventually lead them on to engage themselves in work activities. When elder siblings move onto heavier and more productive work as they grow up, younger siblings generally take up the activities which the elder once were performing earlier.

4

ECONOMIC ACTIVITIES OF CHILDREN: ANALYSIS OF SECONDARY DATA

Available data on child labour from secondary sources has been gathered and analysed in this chapter. The main focus here is on some of the dimensions and determinants of the economic activities of children in rural areas with special reference to India. Evidence is presented with regard to the magnitude, intensity and the nature of activities performed by children. Information regarding wages earned is also given. Selected socio-economic indicators are used to analyse the possible causes of child work participation.

4.1 Data Sources

Data on economic activities of children are rather scarce. Data on the size of child population, dependency ratios and those children who were reported as engaged in any gainful activity is obtained from the decennial censuses of India. Nevertheless, problems arise while comparing these data for different census years because of the definitional changes particularly on work. Problems are also encounted with respect to the reporting of age, occupational classification of children, etc. Labour Enquiry Survey Reports, National Sample Survey Tabulations and Publications of the Bureau of Economics and Statistics are the other major sources of data. A few micro-level studies also have been conducted in the country, but they are all area specific and the scope of these enquiries varies from one to the other. Besides, information is also extracted from some of the micro-level studies conducted in other developing areas of the world.

4.2 Empirical Evidence

About 40 per cent of the population in India comprises of children in the age group 0-14. This young age structure is a consequence of relatively higher levels of fertility and declining mortality. The dependency burden is thus higher especially in the rural areas. The census classification to categorize a person as worker or non-worker does not prescribe any minimum age limit. However, it may be safe to assume that no child under age five is entered as working. Among the child population in rural India nearly one-third are dependents as they belong to the age group of 0-4. Another third of the child population or about half of those aged 5-14 are entered as dependents as shown in Table 4.1. These are the persons who have no activity of their own, but are dependents on other members of the family for their living. Remaining children either go to school or work. It is rather difficult to estimate those who combine schooling and work. The conditions in rural areas are conducive for school-going children to work either by withdrawing from school for a couple of days or intermittently or after school hours. During the last several years the number of children entering school has increased, and as a consequence, the percentage of children working has declined. However, we are not sure whether the proportion of children combining work with schooling has changed over years. One estimate places the percentage of student workers to total child workers at 51 per cent in the case of male and 36 per cent in the case of females in 1961 (Premi, 1973: 72).

The 1971 Census data show that 11.5 per cent of males and 4.6 per cent of females of 5-14 years were full-time workers in rural areas. Considering children performing household duties as those who were engaged in useful activities, the child work participation rate in rural India is estimated to be 13.3 per cent and 22.4 per cent for males and females, respectively. Child work participation rate for girls was thus higher than that for boys. Reciprocally, proportion of full-time school attending girls in the female child population (5-14) is lower than the proportion of full-time school attending boys in the male child population (5-14). This information is presented in Table 4.1. Data presented in the Table show that the ratio of school-going children to the non-school going children is higher for males than for females in both 1961 and 1971 Census.

The 1961 and 1971 Census data on students, dependents and so on presented in Table 4.1 are not strictly comparable due to definitional differences. It is more so with regard to data on work. The 1961 Census data includes marginal workers in the work force whereas the 1971 census data is based on main activity only. Assuming no substantial change in the actual work participation rate of children over 1961-71, the marginal child workers can be estimated to be roughly about 5 per cent for males and 7 per cent for females. Looking at the statistics given for students, children performing household duties, dependents and others in both the censuses, one gets the impression that a bulk of the female marginal workers were children performing household duties and the male marginal workers were students and dependents in 1971 Census. The dependent children (5-14) of 1961 Census refer to those who neither work nor go to school. They perform no other economic activity and are not seeking any work either. The dependent children of 1971 Census on the other hand may be consisting of some marginal workers. However, according to both the censuses 47 per cent of male children and nearly 60 per cent of female children are reported as dependents (see Table 4.1). But we are not sure whether children who neither work nor go to school are absolutely idle. It is possible that a substantial proportion of these children are performing activities which do not come under the purview of the census definition of work or household duty. It is also possible that non-school going marginal workers are under-reported and are counted as dependents. In both the cases certain activities performed by children are concealed.

A meaningful indicator of the incidence of child labour is the child work participation rate. It indicates the magnitude of child labour in relation to the child population. The age-

TABLE 4.1: **Size and Distribution of Child Population in Rural India**

Sex		Child population (0-14) in thousands	Per cent of child population to total population	Per cent of children (0-4) to the total child population (0-14)	Per cent distribution of children (5-14) as					
					Child workers	Students	Children performing household duties	Dependents*	Others@	Total
1971	Males	96,867	43.0	65.9	11.4	36.6	2.0	49.4	0.6	100.0
Census	Females	90,884	42.5	64.3	4.6	19.0	17.8	58.3	0.3	100.0
1961	Males	76,585	41.8	63.9	16.6	35.4	0.3	47.5	0.2	100.0
Census	Females	72,719	41.2	62.1	12.3	14.7	13.2	59.8	0.1	100.0

*Dependents include all non-wokers, even if able bodied, who have no other activity coming under any of the above classification and who are not seeking any work, but are purely dependent.

@ Persons who are not engaged in any activity but are seeking work and those who are with independent means, beggars, vagrants, etc. inmates of penal, mental and charitable institutions are categorised as 'others'.

Sources : 1. Census of India, 1971, *Series 1*, *India*, *Part II—B(i)*, *General Economic Tables*, Controller of Publications, Delhi, 1977: 18-21.

2. Census of India 1971, *Series 1, India, Part II—B(ii), General Economic Tables,* Controller of Publications, Delhi, 1978: 417-423.
3. Census of India, 1971, *Series 1, India, Part II—C(ii), Social and Cultural Tables,* Controller of Publications, Delhi, 1977: 106.
4. Census of India, 1961, *Volume 1, India, Part II—B(i), General Economic Tables,* Manager of Publications, Delhi, 1965: 86-87.
5. Census of India, 1961, *Volume 1, India, Part II—B(iii), General Economic Tables,* Manager of Publications, Delhi, 1965: 590-593.
6. Census of India, 1961, *Volume 1, India, Part II—C(i), Social and Cultural Tables,* Manager of Publications, Delhi, 1965: 408.

specific child work participation rate (child workers to the population of 5-14 years of age, with the assumption that children below five years are not working) shows that according to 1971 Census, the highest participation rate is found in Sikkim (30.7 per cent). Among the major states Andhra Pradesh stands first (16.3 per cent) followed by Karnataka (11.5 per cent), Madhya Pradesh (11.1 per cent), Maharashtra (9.3 per cent), Rajasthan (9.1 per cent), Tamil Nadu (8.6 per cent), Orissa (8.4 per cent), Jammu and Kashmir (6.0 per cent) and so on. Among all the major states child work participation of male children is found to be higher than that of female children.

The sectors engaging children in various economic activities vary from country to country, but child labour is most common in agriculture followed by services and industry. Agricultural child labour constitutes nearly 10 per cent of the total agricultural labour force in the country. In livestock, forestry, fishing, hunting and plantations, they constitute nearly 21 per cent of the total labour force. Children work in all sectors of the economy. In rural areas, about 91.9 per cent of the child labour is found in agricultural sector. Secondary sector makes up 4.6 per cent and service sector 3.5 per cent of the total child workers. Industry-wise classification of child workers is given in Table 4.2.

On the basis of 1971 Census data, fourteen groups of occupations are identified in rural areas as child labour concentrated occupations. Occupations in which more than 25,000 children are engaged-in and which have a child worker-adult worker ratio of more than 3 per cent are considered as child labour concentrated occupations. These data are presented for All India and for Karnataka and Kerala States separately (see Table 4.3).

As was seen in the case of sectoral concentration of child workers, the occupational concentration of child workers also shows the child worker-adult worker ratio, generally, in favour of girls than of boys. This is true for All India as well as for Karnataka and Kerala states. The pattern of occupational concentration of child labour of Karnataka is almost similar to that of All India pattern for both the sexes. For Kerala,

TABLE 4.2 : **Industrial Classification of the Child Workers in Rural India, 1971 Census**

Industrial classification	*Number of child workers*		*Per cent of child workers to the total workers in each category*	
	M	*F*	*M*	*F*
1. Cultivators	3,092,973	748,455	4.6	8.2
2. Agricultural labourers	2,928,901	1,544,584	9.7	10.2
3. Livestock, Forestry, fishing, hunting, Plantations, orchard and allied activities	716,424	138,245	23.5	19.3
4. Mining and quarrying	12,133	7,436	2.4	7.7
5. Household industry	150,520	108,919	4.0	10.9
6. Other than household industry	92,704	48,442	3.1	11.0
7. Construction	24,453	11,172	2.4	10.2
8. Trade and commerce	73,459	8,906	2.9	3.2
9. Transport, storage and communications	10,534	2,481	0.9	5.1
10. Other services	182,560	74,154	2.7	7.8

Source : Census of India, 1971, *Series 1, India, Part II-B (ii) General Economic Tables*, Controller of Publications, Delhi, 1978, 417-423.

TABLE 4.3 : Ratio of Child Workers to Adult Workers in Child Labour Concentrated Occupations* in Rural Areas—1971 Census

Occupational groups (as given in census of India)	*Occupation*	*Per cent child workers (0-14) to adult workers (15+)*					
		India		*Karnataka*		*Kerala*	
		M	*F*	*M*	*F*	*M*	*F*
52	Cooks, waiters, bar tenders and related workers (Domestic and Institutional)	10.8	25.8	10.5	13.7	11.0	33.1
53	Maids and other housekeeping service workers	25.7	21.5	20·8	22.6	30.8	28.4
55	Launders, dry cleaners and pressers	7.1	10.0	5.8	8.1	1.6	1.3
62	Farmers other than cultivators	75.2	123.6	98.4	135.8	1.7	2.0
64	Plantation labourers and related workers	3.0	5.0	6.7	13.4	1.1	2.7
65	Other farm workers	57.3	102.6	101.8	142.8	35.3	26.7
75	Spinners, weavers, knitters, dyers and related workers	4.4	10.0	5.5	12.3	2.3	6.3
77	Food and beverage processors	3.0	5.0	3.8	4.5	1.6	3.1
78	Tobacco preparers and tobacco product makers	10.7	28.4	23.0	41.4	6.4	41.2
79	Tailors, dress makers, sewers, upholsterers and related workers	3.9	6.8	4.7	6.7	1.6	2.1
89	Glass formers, potters and related workers	4.1	8.5	4.6	6.0	2.0	5.1

94	Production and related workers without specific classification	5.6	8.8	7.4	11.3	2.3	4.2
	Cultivators	4.7	8.9	5.7	8.9	0.4	0.8
	Agricultural Labourers	10.7	11.3	14.3	13.9	1.5	2.0

* Occupations in which more than 25,000 children are engaged and which has a child worker-adult worker ratio of more than 3 per cent for All India are considered as child labour concentrated occupations.

Sources : 1. Census of India, 1971, *Series, 1, India, Part II-B (v), General Economic Tables*, Controller of Publications, Delhi, 1978 : 393-692.

2. Census of India, 1971, *Series 14, Mysore, Part II-B (iii) Economic Tables*, Controller of Publications, New Delhi, 1979 : 425-610.

3. Census of India, 1971, *Series 9, Kerala, Part II-B (ii), Economic Tables*, Controller of Publications, New Delhi, 1977 : 262-367.

however, higher concentration is found only in four groups of occupations, *viz.* other farm workers, maids and other house-keeping service workers, cooks, waiters, bar-tenders and related workers and tobacco preparers and tobacco product makers (see Table 4.3). Thus, unlike All India and Karnataka patterns, the highest concentration of child workers of Kerala is found in service sector.

Generally, wage employment and schooling are competitive for children both in agriculture and non-agricultural occupations. In the case of self-employment or working at home to help other members of the household, schooling and work can be combined. In beedi rolling, for example, working and schooling can be combined as beedi rolling work is usually carried out in the household itself and there are no rigid working hours or working norms that have to be met. Similar is the case in occupations such as spinning, weaving, dress making, etc.

A major concentration of working children in rural areas is in livestock rearing. Though not proportionate, generally in areas where relatively larger number of livestock are raised the child work participation is found to be high. In states like Rajasthan, Karnataka, Madhya Pradesh, Andhra Pradesh, Orissa and Jammu and Kashmir, both the number of livestock raised and the number of children working per household are much higher compared to Kerala, Tamil Nadu, Uttar Pradesh, West Bengal, Assam and Tripura.

The Report of the Rural Labour Enquiry Survey (Government of India, 1965) conducted during 1963-65 provides information for the number of days worked per annum by children in the agricultural labour households and all rural labour households. When the major portion of the household income was derived from the wage paid manual labour they were categorised as rural labour households. According to this report childern in rural labour households were working on an average for 267 days per year out of which 187 days were accounted for by wage employment. In agricultural labour households separately, the corresponding figures were 280 days and 202 days. Non-agricultural child labourers were found to be working more number of days than the agricultural child labourers and self-employed and salaried children. These data separately for agricultural labour households and rural labour households are presented in Table 4.4.

The Survey Report provides state-wise statistics for the intensity of child work. Data show state-wise variation in the intensity of work performed by children in terms of number of days employed per annum. In West Bengal agricultural and non-agricultural child labourers of both agricultural labour and all rural labour households worked for about 320 days in a year. In Gujarat, Punjab-Haryana and Jammu and Kashmir, children who were working as agricultural labourers worked for about three-fourth of a year. Karnataka, Kerala, Punjab-Haryana and West Bengal are bracketed for the highest number of days worked by non-agricultural child labourers among agricultural labour households and Assam, Bihar, Punjab-Haryana, Kerala and West Bengal among all rural labour households.

With respect to educational variables that affect participation of children in different kinds of work we have to consider literacy and educational levels of population, schooling of children, school drop-outs and wastage and availability of schooling facilities. The literacy levels of adult population is a good indicator of the levels of enrolment of children in schools. Illiteracy among the population particularly among females acts as a major deterrent to school enrolment of children. When schooling is denied they are usually forced to work.

Data for Karnataka State have been presented in Table 4.5 to show the negative relationship between illiteracy among general population and schooling of children. For both sexes this relationship was found highly significant. Higher illiteracy in the general population of Karnataka State showed higher child work participation for males (r=.728*) whereas with respect to females the general illiteracy increased the participation of girls in household duties (r=.831*) rather than in the directly productive activities. The direct relationship between

* Significant at 1 per cent level.

TABLE 4.4: **Employment and Unemployment of Usually Occupied@ Children in Terms of Estimated Number of Full Days, in 1964-65**

Usual occupation	*Average number of days worked in*					*Average number of days not worked*			
	Wage employment basis	*Employment on salary basis*	*Self employment*	*Unclassified*	*Total*	*Due to sickness, bad weather, etc.*	*Due to want of work*	*Unclassified*	*Total*
Agricultural Households									
Agricultural labourers	224	N	22	14	260	11	62	19	92
Non-agricultural labourers	190	N	66	57	313	3	23	12	38
Other Occupations*	25	7	255	2	289	10	4	8	22
All Occupations	202	1	62	15	280	10	51	17	78
All Rural Labour Households									
Agricultural labourers	223	N	22	14	259	11	63	18	92

Non-agricultural labourers	212	N	51	34	297	13	30	10	53
Other Occupations*	26	8	247	1	282	14	9	8	31
All Occupations	187	2	64	14	267	11	50	17	78

Notes : The total number of days of columns 6 and 10 falls short of 365 days due to the fact that the days of partial activities have not been taken into account.

N = nil

* = Includes self employed and salaried persons

@ = The usual occupation of a child was the gainful occupation which he/she usually pursued.

Source : Government of India, Ministry of Labour, *Rural Labour Enquiry, 1963-65*, Final Report, Simla, 1965: 154.

TABLE 4.5: **Educational Levels of the General Population, School Enrolment of Children, Educational Wastage and Child Work Participation in Karnataka**

District	Per cent illiterate to the total population 1971		Per cent school going children to the total child population (5-14) 1971		Educational wastages among children in classes I-VIII (1964-75)		No. of high schools per 10,000 children (5-14)	Per cent children (5-14) performing household duties, 1971		Child work participation rate (5-14), 1971	
	M	F	M	F	M	F		M	F	M	F
1	2	3	4	5	6	7	8	9	10	11	12
Bangalore	48.7	66.7	52.0	39.7	53	63	3.0	1.2	15.8	10.1	2.9
Belgaum	57.5	81.7	45.4	25.6	81	91	2.3	1.5	25.3	15.5	5.6
Bellary	64.7	85.4	34.7	19.0	81	91	2.1	3.4	20.8	16.5	8.7
Bidar	69.1	91.3	35.1	11.9	84	95	2.3	6.2	31.5	13.9	3.1
Bijapur	59.7	85.7	46.9	21.4	83	94	1.9	1.5	25.1	16.7	6.5

Chickmagalur	56.1	74.6	45.1	29.5	75	87	2.5	3.4	18.0	10.7	4.6
Chitradurga	58.0	79.8	40.5	23.2	80	90	2.5	7.3	22.1	16.4	8.3
Coorg	49.8	62.2	51.5	44.7	67	70	4.2	1.8	7.9	10.5	7.9
Dharwar	48.7	75.0	49.3	31.4	83	91	2.4	1.6	22.1	15.9	7.0
Gulbarga	71.3	91.4	30.4	12.3	88	96	1.8	4.3	28.1	17.0	4.6
Hassan	58.9	80.3	40.4	30.5	80	91	2.4	3.1	22.9	13.8	3.6
Kolar	63.4	82.9	41.6	24.0	78	89	2.0	1.8	20.5	15.3	7.1
Mandya	68.4	86.9	34.2	18.2	80	90	2.1	1.3	26.0	16.3	3.4
Mysore	66.8	82.4	34.7	22.4	78	88	2.1	2.2	21.6	14.7	3.0
Uttara Kannada	50.4	68.7	54.3	39.6	77	83	4.7	2.5	16.0	9.2	3.2
Raichur	69.1	90.7	30.1	11.9	88	96	1.6	8.8	32.2	18.7	8.1
Shimoga	54.4	73.1	46.5	32.2	75	86	2.3	2.6	19.9	11.3	3.7

(Contd.)

1	2	3	4	5	6	7	8	9	10	11	12
Dakshina Kannada	47.7	65.0	58.1	43.1	71	73	2.9	1.5	8.7	8.1	10.9
Tumkur	60.1	81.7	43.7	26.2	74	87	2.7	2.0	22.3	14.6	4.2

Sources :
1. Census of India, 1971, Mysore, *Series 14, Part I—A, Volume II, General Report*, Controller of Publications, Delhi, 1975: 588.
2. Census of India, 1971, Mysore, Series 14, Part II—B (i), *Economic Tables*, Controller of Publications, Delhi, 1974: 105-569.
3. Census of India, 1971, Mysore, *Series 14, Part II—B (ii), Economic Tables*, Controller of Publications, Delhi, 1980: 423-441.
4. Census of India, 1971, Mysore, *Series 14, Part II—C (ii), Social and Cultural Tables and Fertility Tables*, Delhi, 1980: 82-115.
5. Rajeshwari Chandrashekaran, *A Critical Study in Depth of the Various Measures Taken by the Government of Karnataka (Mysore) in the Field of Primary Education during the Period, 1947-1972*, Unpublished Doctoral Thesis, Institute for Social and Economic Change, Bangalore, 1978: 103.
6. Government of Karnataka, Bureru of Economics and Statistics, *Statistical Abstract of Karnataka: 1973-74*, Bangalore, 1975: 150.0.

illiteracy and child work participation was found at micro level as well. A study conducted in rural Uttar Pradesh of India showed absolute illiteracy among the parents of more than 80 per cent of children engaged in work (Sawhney, 1979: 208).

Since independence school enrolment of children has been improving for both sexes in the country. School enrolment ratio which stood at 65 per cent for boys in 1953-54 rose to 76 per cent in 1958-59, further to 96 per cent in 1968-69, and 100 per cent in 1975-76. The corresponding figures for girls were 28, 38, 59 and 66 per cent respectively (Government of India, 1962: 300; Government of India, 1980: 20-22). However, school enrolment may not be uniform among all sections of the population. School enrolment of children among weaker sections in the rural areas are definitely on the lower side. The difference between the school enrolment ratios of scheduled population and general population widened from primary school to high school (Rayappa and Grover, 1980: 27-28). Enrolment ratios of male and female children are also not the same.

Even though school enrolment ratios may be high, school retention rates may not be so. This has been amply demonstrated by the amount of wastage in school education particularly in rural areas. The wastage rate which was as high as 60 per cent for primary stage in the country in 1958-59 (Government of India, 1962: 301) has not shown any improvement even after more than ten years. In fact, it has worsened to 66.9 per cent in 1970-71 (Government of India, 1977: 20). The higher the school wastage, the higher the chance of children participating in economic activities. The data presented in Table 4 5 for the districts of Karnataka brings out a high positive correlation between these two variables for both boys and girls.*

* For boys, the correlation co-efficient between wastage rate and work participation rate was found to be .726. In the case of girls the relation between wastage and participation rate in household duties was found very significant (r=.840). In both the cases the correlation coefficient is statistically significant at 1 per cent level.

5

NEED FOR AND THE METHODOLOGY OF PRIMARY INVESTIGATION

5.1 Need for Primary Investigation

The need for primary data for investigating the dimensions, causes and consequences of child work participation is deeply felt especially in the Indian context. This conclusion is arrived at after an analysis of available data on the topic from secondary sources. The following paragraphs provide reasons for the collection of primary data for this study.

From the available secondary data, it was not possible to distinguish among children as those who go to school but do not work, those who go to school as well as work, those who work but do not go to school and those who neither go to school nor work. This information is of paramount importance for an indepth analysis of work participation of children due to the reasons mentioned earlier in the text. Moreover, the concept of work needs to be given a broader connotation than what has been generally understood from a purely economic point of view. Encompassing in the definition of work certain activities children perform on the family farm, in family business or elsewhere, which do not come under the purview of the general definition of child labour would help us in examining the economic value of children to their parents.

In the Indian context, child work participation has to be studied by socio-economic and educational groups, for, differentials are expected in the magnitude and intensity of child work participation among these groups. Secondary data for such an analysis are lacking and hence the present study necessitates collection of background information of working children at household level such as religion, caste, income, land and other asset ownership, educational level of the members of the household, etc. This would be useful in identifying the various factors (causes) determining child work participation. Besides, need for information with respect to the consequences of work participation of children also necessitates a primary investigation.

5.2 Data Requirements

The overall data requirements for primary investigation come under five categories, namely:

(a) Data identifying children as those who go to school but do not work, those who work but do not go to school, those who combine schooling and work and those who do neither.

(b) Data on the dimensions of child activities such as the magnitude, intensity, place of work and their direct earnings.

(c) Background information required to analyse the various causes of child work participation such as caste, religion, family size, family income, educational status of the members of the household, size of the cultivated land-holding, animal wealth and occupational status of the members of the household.

(d) Data on school attendance, school performance, schooling facility, children's contribution to family income, etc. to explain the consequences of child work participation.

(e) Parents' attitude towards child work participation, their perceptions of the support that they may receive in future from children and their educational aspirations for children.

Field work was undertaken to collect the above-mentioned information at household and village levels.

5.3 Data Collecting Instruments

Pre-designed and pre-tested interview schedule was the data collecting instrument used at the household level. The interview schedule was divided into three parts, namely,

(a) Household Schedule,
(b) Economic Activity Sheet for Children,
(c) Schedule to Collect information regarding parents' attitude.

Household schedule was designed to collect information regarding individual and household characteristics required for detailed analysis such as family size, age, sex, occupation and educational status of each member of the household, caste, land holding size, income, etc. This information was collected from the head or any responsible person of the household. The 'Economic Activity Sheet' was developed to elicit information regarding work input of children. Data on the various activities children perform and the place of their work were also collected through the 'Economic Activity Sheet'. The 'Economic Activity Sheet' was restricted to children of six to fifteen years of age and was canvassed for each child falling under the above mentioned age group. The schedule containing attitudinal questions was developed in such a way that interviewees' attitude towards child work participation, their perceptions of support from children in future and their aspirations of educating their off-springs could be collected in detail. The attitudinal schedule was canvassed for women aged 20 to 45 years only.

5.4 Area of Study

The area selected for study is the rural area of Dakshina Kannada district. It is a coastal district of Karnataka State, bordering Kerala State in the South and consisting of eight taluks and 663 villages. This district is one of the most developed districts in Karnataka State. The twenty-two socio-economic indicators used in the Draft Sixth Five-Year Plan to rank the nineteen districts in the State according to their socio-economic development indicate that during 1971-72,

1974-75, 1976-77 and 1979-80 Dakshina Kannada ranked second in the list (Government of Karnataka, 1980: 86-89). The highest level of literacy in the State is found in this district (53 per cent according to 1981 Census). Women in this district are economically more active. Their work participation rate is the highest in the State (32 per cent according to 1981 Census). 'Tulu' dialect is spoken by majority of people.

Dakshina Kannada receives very good monsoon. Irrigation is provided mainly by streams and rivulets. Very good rainfall and irrigation facilities make double cropping common in the district. Yet a large proportion of workers are engaged in household manufacturing. While the proportion of workers engaged in household manufacturing in other districts of Karnataka State ranges from 1.3 per cent to 6.5 per cent in 1981, in Dakshina Kannada district it captures nearly 19 per cent of the total workers. The predominant occupation coming under household manufacturing in Dakshina Kannada district is beedi rolling. Beedi rolling is a child labour intensive industry. In Dakshina Kannada district, it is the single occupation in which the largest proportion of child workers are engaged. The nature of operations involved in beedi rolling is such that children can combine schooling and work without affecting school attendance.

Since one of the objectives of this study is to look into the circumstances promoting compatibility of schooling with work, the selection of Dakshina Kannada district as the area of study is justified, for, beedi rolling activity is extensively prevalent there. From among the eight taluks in the district, Buntwal taluk and subsequently one of the eighty-four villages in that taluk namely Munnur was selected for the household survey on the basis of the highest percentage of workers engaged in household industry. It was, however, realized that data only from a situation which is conducive for children to combine schooling with work will not serve the objectives of the study. Data were needed from other situations as well for comparison purposes. Hence two more villages were selected where per cent workers engaged in household industry is quite small. However, the main criterion for selecting these two villages was the adequacy of schooling facility as that being one of the hypothesized causes of non-participation of children in work.

Due to recent developments in education almost every village in Dakshina Kannada district is provided with atleast one primary school. Although there are many villages in the district which do not have high schools, children of most of these villages have proximity to a high school either on foot or by transport. Hence it was decided to take distance and transport facility to the nearest high school as a proxy for adequate schooling facility. The next task was to select a village without high school facility and having the maximum distance to the nearest high school and another having high school facility within the village. While selecting the first type of village it was kept in mind that there was no adequate transport facility to commute to the high school every day. Due to inadequacy of data to select villages with the above-mentioned characteristics the selection was accomplished through consultation with the Block Development Officers. Ultimately, a remote village without high school facility—Neriya—in Belthangady taluk and another with a high school situated within the village, namely, Ajjavara in Sullia taluk were selected along with Munnur in Buntwal taluk for final household survey. Thus the selection of the villages can be said to be purposive. The socio-economic characteristics of the three villages selected for the household survey are given in Table 5.1.

5.5 Selection of Households

Simple random sampling technique was used to select households for the survey. The sample size was pre-fixed to 100 households in each village due to various constraints. One ward in each village was selected for our purpose. While in Ajjavara and Neriya villages, wards having the highest concentration of the Scheduled Castes and Scheduled Tribes were taken to get a fair proportion of scheduled population in the sample, there was no specific criterion for selecting the ward in Munnur.

5.6 Quality of the Data

To the extent difficulties were encountered in data collection,

TABLE 5.1: **Socio-Economic and Demographic Characteristics of the Selected Villages, 1971 Census**

Characteristics	*Ajjavara*	*Munnur*	*Neriya*
1. Area in acres	6,029	1,743	26,817
2. Total population	3,808	3,946	3,212
3. Number of households	622	536	497
4. Average number of persons per household	631	7.4	6.5
5. Per cent SC population	22.4	1.5	4.7
6. Per cent ST population	8.9	1.4	12.3
7. Per cent literates in the population	33.7	30.4	40.1
8. Number of Primary and Middle schools in the village*	2	2	4
9. High school facility in the village*	1	nil	nil
10. Distance to the nearest high school from the village*	within the village	0.5 to 2 kms	13 to 20 kms
11. % of workers in the population	33.5	46.6	37.8
12. % cultivators to the total workers	34.5	17.0	32.8
13. % Agricultural labourers to the total workers	46.4	16.8	32.2
14. % engaged in household industry to the total workers	7.1	51.2	3.0

* Information based on primary data.

the collected data has suffered in its quality. As the reference period fixed for the study was the year preceding the interview date recall lapse also affected the quality of data to some extent. It is not possible in a study of this type to test the quality of the data collected. However, the general quality of the data can be guaged by comparing the collected data with similar data from secondary sources. Nevertheless, the quality of work and other background data cannot be tested since comparable data with similar definition from secondary sources is not available. The age data is of course, compared with that obtained from the censuses. This has been presented in Table 5.2.

TABLE 5.2 : **Comparison of Survey Data with Census Data**

		Census Data (Dakshina Kannada, Rural)*	*Survey Data (1982)*
1.	% children (0-5) in the total population	17.74	17.27
2.	% children (6-15) in the total population	28.44	27.28
3.	% females (20-45) in the total population	33.35	13.94
4.	Sex ratio of the population	996	987

* Census data for items 1, 2 and 3 are taken from 1971 Census. For item 4, census data are obtained from 1981 Census. Sex ratio computed from the census data corresponds to the taluks from which villages for the field study are selected.

The proportion of children (0-5 and 6-15) and females aged 20-45 obtained from the total population of the field data are almost the same as that computed from census data. Even the sex ratio does not differ much. Of course, some change in the age distribution of the population is bound to take place over years. The comparison of age data of the study with census data, thus, indicates that the general quality of the data collected for this study is more or less satisfactory.

5.7 Population of the Study

The study is limited to children 6-15 years of age. Age is defined in terms of completed years. Since the reference period fixed for the study was the year preceding the day of interview, information collected for those who had recently completed six years refer to their period before completing six years as well. The lower age limit of six was set on the assumption that normally children below six years are neither physically nor mentally capable of working. Moreover, in Karnataka, five years and ten months is the minimum age fixed for enrolling in primary schools. Assuming no repetition in schools, a child who joined First standard when he was six years is expected to be in Tenth standard by his sixteenth year.

Besides child population, the study also consists of female population aged 20-45 to whom the attitudinal schedules were canvassed. Females were selected for the attitudinal questions because it is widely known that in Dakshina Kannada district, wives have a say in the decisions taken in any matter concerning their children. Females of 20-45 years are those who are in the reproductive age group and thus include both mothers and prospective mothers.

5.8 Method of Analysis

Analyses of data are mostly descriptive. Percentage analyses and association techniques are used to analyse the data. Association techniques used include correlation technique and the non-parametric test, *viz.* chi-square test. Chi-square test is used to find out the association between the background variable and the work-school status of children.

6

DIMENSIONS OF CHILD ACTIVITIES: INSIGHTS FROM PRIMARY INVESTIGATION

In this chapter an elaborate description of the dimensions of child activities in terms of magnitude, intensity, wages and place of work based on primary data is presented. The chapter begins with an account of the child population of the sample and its sex and age composition. Next the definitional difference of child work participation rates is dealt with. It is followed by a discussion on the compatibility and/or competitiveness of schooling and work. Finally an account of the participation of children in households chores and the activities they perform simultaneously is given.

6.1 Composition of the Child Population

About 45 per cent of the population enumerated in a sample of 285 households selected for the study constitute children who were aged 0-15 years. Thus, out of 2049 persons in the sample, 913 persons are children who had not completed 16 years of age at the time of interview. Among the three villages selected for the study, Munnur has got a higher dependent population than both Neriya and Ajjavara. As could be seen in Table 6.1, unlike in the other two villages, in Munnur the proportion of girls in the female population is found to be more than the proportion of boys in the male population.

The child work participation refers only to those children who are between 6-15 years of age. The sample population of the study constitutes about 27 per cent children who are between the ages under reference. Data presented in Table 6.1 show that 27 per cent of those aged 6-15 years who are 559 in number account for 61 per cent of the total child population (0-15). Thus 39 children among every 100 of 0-15 years were below 6 years of age. They amount to 17 per cent of the total population. Looking at the village-wise data presented in Table 6.1, it is clear that while the broad age composition of the child population in Neriya and Ajjavara are almost similar, Munnur has got comparatively more children below age six for every 100 persons in the population.

For the purpose of analysis, in this study, children (6-15) have been grouped into four mutually exclusive categories according to work and school status. This is presented in Table 6.2. The Table shows that about 38 per cent boys and 34 per cent girls in the selected villages attend school without getting themselves engaged in any work either intermittently or after school hours or during school vacation. Another 26 per cent boys and 17 per cent girls combine schooling with work. Rest of them are workers who do not attend school and those who do neither. Data indicate that 16 per cent boys and 23 per cent girls are children who are working without attending school. Remaining 20 per cent boys and 26 per cent girls neither work nor attend school.

An important finding emerging from this study as shown in Table 6.2 is that the proportion of children who neither go to school nor work is quite significant. Nearly 20 per cent boys and 26 per cent girls fall in this category. In the sample, highest proportion of them is found in village Ajjavara (32 per cent boys and 40 per cent girls) followed by Munnur (18 per cent boys and 23 per cent girls) and Neriya (10 per cent boys and 17 per cent girls). These are discussed in the next chapter.

Children aged 6-15 years are sub-divided into three age groups, *viz*. 6-8 years, 9-11 years and 12-15 years. Out of 559 children (6-15) being studied, 29 per cent are in the first age group, another 29 per cent in the second and the remaining

TABLE 6.1 : **Size and Composition of the Child Population**

Village	*Total population*		*Child population (0-15)*		*Child population (6-15)*		*Per cent of child population (0-15) to the total population*		*Per cent of child population (6-15) to the total population*		*Per cent of child population (6-15) to the total child population (0-15)*	
	M	*F*	*M*	*F*	*M*	*F*	*M*	*F*	*M*	*F*	*M*	*F*
Neriya	318	332	145	138	89	88	45.6	41.6	28.0	26.5	61.4	63.8
Munnur	396	396	185	190	105	111	46.7	48.0	26.5	28.0	56.8	58.4
Ajjavara	317	290	140	115	89	77	44.2	39.7	28.1	26.6	63.8	67.0
Total	1031	1018	470	443	283	276	45.6	43.5	27.5	27.1	60.2	62.3

TABLE 6.2: **Work-School Status of Children (6-15) in the Selected Villages**

Village	*Total child population (6-15)*		*Per cent children who are attending school but not working*		*Per cent children who are attending school as well as working*		*Per cent children who are working but are not attending school*		*Per cent children who are neither working nor attending school*		*Child work participation rate including those who combine schooling and work*		*Participation rate of children in any activity including those who perform household duties*	
	M	*F*	*M*	*F*	*M*	*F*	*M*	*F*	*M*	*F*	*M*	*F*	*M*	*F*
Neriya	89	88	29.2	42.1	37.1	22.7	23.6	18.2	10.1	17.0	60.7	40.9	80.9	93.2
Munnur	105	111	38.1	22.5	26.7	20.7	17.1	33.3	18.1	23.4	43.8	54.1	61.0	76.6
Ajjavara	89	77	47.2	41.6	14.6	3.9	6.7	14.3	31.5	40.3	21.4	18.2	48.3	59.7
Total	283	276	38.2	34.1	26.2	16.7	15.9	23.2	19.8	26.1	42.1	39.9	63.3	77.2

42 per cent belong to the third. Thus a large proportion of those aged 6-15 years are in the high school going age group. Females outnumber males in the age group 9-11 years, whereas in the other two age groups sex ratio is in favour of males.

Table 6.3 gives the percentage distribution of children (6-15) in study villages in each work-school status category by age group. As it is evident from the Table, in age group 6-8, children are concentrated in two categories, *viz.* those who are attending school and not working and those who are neither working nor attending school. More than 40 per cent of children of both the sexes belong to each of these categories. Working children in this age group are too small in number. As the children grow up, they move out of the last category, that is, complete idleness. First, most of them start attending school and then gradually they drop out and participate in labour force. The table shows that in age group 9-11 nearly 55 per cent boys and 47 per cent girls attend school without participating in work. Another 27 per cent boys and 19 per cent girls are combining schooling and work. In all, 82 per cent boys and 65 per cent girls in this age group are attending school. In the next age group of 12-15, the proportion of those who attend school without participating in work comes down to 25 per cent and 17 per cent, for boys and girls respectively. Those who combine schooling and work, however, goes up to 39 per cent among boys and 26 per cent among girls. Another 30 per cent boys and 45 per cent girls are those who participate in work without attending school. Remaining 6 per cent of boys and 13 per cent of girls are those who do neither.

One can infer from the data presented in Table 6.3 that, most of the children who are idle when they are in the age group 6-8 enroll in schools when they enter the age group of 9-11. Some of them combine schooling and work and others do not. When they move on to the age group of 12-15, many who belong to the first category—those who attend school and do not work—either combine schooling with work or drop out from school to work An initial increase and then a decline in the proportion of children in this category by age group is thus

TABLE 6.3: **Work-School Status of Children by Age Group**

Age group	*Total number of children (6-15)*		*Per cent children who are attending school but not working*		*Per cent children who are attending school and also working*		*Per cent children who are working but not attending school*		*Per cent children who are neither working nor attending school*	
	M	*F*	*M*	*F*	*M*	*F*	*M*	*F*	*M*	*F*
6—8	81	80	43.2	43.8	4.9	2.5	6.2	2.5	45.7	51.6
9—11	77	86	54.6	46.5	27.3	18.6	5.2	15.1	13.0	19.8
12—15	125	110	24.8	17.3	39.2	25.5	29.6	44.6	6.4	12.7
Total	283	276	38.2	34.1	26.6	16.7	15.9	23.2	19.8	26.1

observed. In the case of those who combine schooling and work and those who work without attending school, the proportion of children by age group consistently increases for both the sexes. On the other hand the proportion of children who are idle declines consistently by age for both the sexes. Some of these idle children seem to enter work force, as they grow up, without ever enrolling in schools.

6.2 Definition of Child Work Participation

At the very outset definitional clarity is required before going into details of child work participation. This would help us to understand the differences in child work participation rates due to changes in the definitions employed. It has been widely pronounced that official data regarding child work participation are under estimates especially in developing countries (Goddard and White, 1982). Special care was taken in this study to identify those child workers who are usually overlooked. Consequently, work participation rate of children in this study is expected to be much higher than the rates given by official data.

The 1961 and 1971 Censuses of India define a 'worker' as a person who participate in economically productive activities by his physical or mental capacity. The 1971 Census count of workers is based on main activity whereas the 1961 Census definition includes even marginal workers. The present study adheres to 1961 Census definition of a 'worker' and thus includes even marginal workers in the definition. Activities such as planting in the kitchen garden; watering plants; scaring birds and animals which destroy crops; picking, spreading and peeling arecanuts; tying rolled beedies; shaping beedi leaves, etc. are regarded as directly productive activities in the study. These are generally not reported as work by parents and are often overlooked in the official count. It was experienced that only probing could help in identifying such activities performed by children.

The 1971 Census adopted a week preceding the interview as the reference period for regular activities and the year preceding the interview as the reference period for seasonal activities. For the 1961 Census, preceding fortnight was the reference period used for regular activities. In the case of seasonal activities, if the person had had some regular work of more than one hour a day throughout the greater part of the working season, he or she was counted as a worker. Thus a minimum of one hour work a day was set in the 1961 Census definition of a worker for seasonal activities. The 1971 Census definition does not have any such minimum. In the present study, as in the 1961 Census, the minimum of one hour work a day is included in the definition. Besides, it includes one more clause of a minimum of 20 days of work in the year under reference. Thus all those children who have performed at least any one of the economically productive activities for not less than an hour per day and for a minimum of 20 days in the year preceding the interview are considered as workers. This definition is used both for regular activities and for seasonal activities alike. Hence the difference in the reference period used and the minimum set by the 1961 Census and the present study has to be noted. Undoubtedly, the definition used in this study in much broader than the one used in the 1961 Census. The broader reference period used have added more children to the work force.

Data on child workers in the censuses of India are given for the age-interval 0-14 years whereas in the present study the upper age limit is fixed as fifteen years. This increment in the upper age limit has resulted in a substantial increase in child work participation rates, for, work participation rate tends to increase as the age increases. Moreover, due to age preference many of those who are sixteen and seventeen years might have reported their age as fifteen years and as a result, indirectly workers among them have also been recorded for this study. Due to above-mentioned reasons, child work participation in the present study is bound to be much higher than the rates computed from census data for the taluks to which the selected villages belong. Table 6.2 presents work participation of children in the three villages.

Work participation rates of children in this study are calculated under three definitions. In the first instance, participation rates are computed without including those who combine schooling and work in the work force. Later on, they are clubbed to find out the work participation rate separately. Finally, those who perform household duties are also considered as those who are engaged in useful activities and corresponding participation rates in any economic activities are computed. Table 6.2 shows that about 16 per cent of boys and 23 per cent of girls in rural Dakshina Kannada are workers who do not attend school. Among boys, highest participation rates are found in Neriya (village with inadequate high school facility) followed by Munnur (beedi rolling activity dominated village) and Ajjavara (village with a high school) whereas among girls the sequence is Munnur, Neriya and Ajjavara. When those children who combine schooling and work are included in the total child work force, the work participation rate shoots up to 42 per cent among boys and 40 per cent among girls. Village-wise pattern of the work participation rates are found to be the same as that of the earlier case for both the sexes.

Sex differentials are observed in the work participation rates of all the three villages. While in Neriya and Ajjavara, it was found to be higher among boys in the beedi rolling activity dominated village, *viz.* Munnur, girls have higher participation rates than boys. If we consider household duties as economic activities, participation rates of children in any economic activities become comparatively higher among girls in all the three villages. In rural Dakshina Kannada, participation rates for male and female children in the work force with this definition work out to 63 per cent and 77 per cent respectively.

Regardless of all the differences in the definitions, a comparison of child work participation rates observed in the study can be made to the ones computed from census data. Leaving apart the difference in the reference period and the minimum set, the 1971 Census data which based on main activity correspond to the rates calculated in the study without including children who combine schooling and work.* On the other hand, participation rates referring to all the workers

---

* Proportion of marginal workers among those who work without attending school is negligible.

except those who are engaged in household duties without performing any other productive activities correspond to the 1961 Census rates which is inclusive of main as well as marginal workers. The 1971 Census data show that 10 per cent of male children and 13 per cent of female children (5-14) are full-time workers in rural Dakshina Kannada against the rates of 16 per cent for male and 23 per cent for female children (6-15) in this study. When the 1961 Census data are compared with the primary data, the difference in the rates becomes very significant, the rates being around 17 per cent in the census against about 40 per cent in this study. The substantial variation is due to definitional differences and the under-estimates in the censuses. One can, therefore, infer that a sizeable proportion of marginal child workers are not returned as workers in the official count.

6.3 Compatibility and Competitiveness of Schooling and Work

In the earlier sections two types of child workers are identified in terms of school and work status. In one situation schooling and work are compatible and in the other they are competitive. In this section, variations in the intensity of work and activities performed by these two types of child workers are illustrated.

Compatibility of schooling and work is possible in three ways. Schooling can be combined with work after school hours, intermittently and during school vacation. In this study, only the first and third modes of schooling and work combination are recorded. Withdrawing from schools to work during peak seasons or as and when the need arises was not reported. If this is true, the impact of work on schooling would not be reflected on the school attendance of these children. Table 6.4 depicts how children in rural Dakshina Kannada combine work and schooling.

Wage labourers among school-going children are very few in number. It could be observed from the Table that school-going children who work for wages, do so during school vacation. Compatibility of beedi rolling activities and unpaid farm activities with schooling is possible even by way of working during out-of-school hours. Not all of them do

TABLE 6.4 : Mode of Compatibility of Schooling and Work by Children

Mode of compatibility	*Combining Schooling and Work*					
	for wages		*on the family farm*		*in beedi industry*	
	M	*F*	*M*	*F*	*M*	*F*
Working during school vacation	5 (100.0)	4 (100.0)	40 (100.0)	15 (100.0)	30 (100.0)	24 (100.0)
Working after school hours	0 (0.0)	0 (0.0)	34 (85.0)	12 (80.0)	30 (100.0)	24 (100.0)
N	5	4	40	15	30	24

Note : Figures in the parantheses refer to percentages.

work after school hours on the family farm. As shown in the Table, 15 per cent of boys and 20 per cent of girls in the 'school-going unpaid family farm child workers' category have not reported combination of work with schooling during out-of-school hours. In beedi rolling industry, however, 100 per cent of school-going child workers reported both the modes of child work combination.

It has been found that children who combine work with schooling either work for wages or on the family farm or in the household industry. More than 95 per cent of them were reported as unpaid family workers. Majority of school-going male child workers work on the family farm (53 per cent) whereas a large proportion of girls combine beedi rolling with schooling (56 per cent). When we look at the data displayed in Table 6.5, a distinct variation in the intensity of work performed by school-going children by nature of activities emerges. The table shows that children who work only during school vacation work for less number of days and hours per year than who work after school hours. School-going children who work in the beedi industry engage themselves in work, on an average, for about 240 days per year whereas wage labourers who work only during school vacation engage themselves for about 70 days. On the family farm, they work for 143 days.

Girls work for less number of days per year than boys in agriculture as well as in beedi rolling activities. Considering the work-input in terms of hours worked per day, a lot of variation is noticed between wage labour and family labour among children who combine schooling and work. Within the category of those who combine schooling and work, children working for wages have to work on an average eight hours per day while children working on their own family farm do not work for more than three hours. In beedi rolling, school attending working children spend on an average, more than three hours per day. A comparison of work-input data presented in Table 6.5 by nature of work reveals that school-going children spend more time in beedi rolling activities than in farm activities. In farm activities, boys work for more number of hours per day than girls and in beedi rolling activities girls spend more time than boys.

TABLE 6.5 : **Child Work Intensity by Work-School Status**

	Working but not attending school						*Combining schooling and work*				
	for wages		*on the family farm*		*in beedi industry*		*for* wages*	*on the family farm*		*in beedi industry*	
	M	*F*	*M*	*F*	*M*	*F*	*M+F*	*M*	*F*	*M*	*F*
Average number of days worked per year	206	150	270	156	282	274	69	154	120	250	227
Average number of hours worked per day	8.5	8.3	5.1	3.5	7.8	7.6	8.0	2.7	2.4	2.9	3.1
Per cent participation to the total in the broad category	31.1	21.9	31.1	18.8	37.8	59.4	—	52.3	34.9	40.0	55.8
N	14	14	14	12	17	38	9	40	15	30	24

*Since N is less than 10, means have not been calculated separately.

In rural Dakshina Kannada, the highest concentration of child workers who do not attend school is found to be in beedi industry (38 per cent boys and 59 per cent girls). Compared to those who work on the family farm or for wages, beedi rollers work for maximum number of days per year. When we consider the time-input data, it is clear that children working for wages have lengthier days of work than family workers. Girls work on an equal footing with boys in wage employment and in beedi industry. They work relatively less number of hours than boys on the family farm (3.5 hours per day by girls against 5.1 hours per day by boys). Generally, among the full-time workers in farm, off-farm and wage employment, boys work for more number of days per year than girls.

When a comparison of work-input in terms of days worked per year and hours worked per day between those who combine schooling with work and those who do not is made, a higher intensity of work among the latter group of children is affirmed. In wage employment, while full-time child workers work for more than 150 days per year school-going children work only for about 70 days. Though wage earning non-school going child workers put in more time to work per day than wage earning school attending child worker, the difference is not considerable. In both the cases, children work for as many as eight hours a day. Like in wage employment, higher intensity of work among non-school going child workers compared to school-going child workers is noticed on the family farm as well as in household industry. This is true for both the sexes. This information is presented in Table 6.5. Thus in situations where work and schooling are competitive, children work for more number of days per year and more number of hours per day than in situations where work and schooling are compatible. This is due to the lack of time available at the disposal of school-going children which can be utilized for work contribution. Of course, when work is compatible with schooling by working during school vacation, children get sufficient time to engage themselves in work for a longer period. More time-input by school-going child workers in wage employment which is generally performed during school vacation is an evidence of the influence of availability of disposable time on work.

Non-school-going child workers can be dichotomously categorised on the basis of their educational status, *viz.*

(i) those who had never been enrolled, and
(ii) those who had been enrolled but dropped out.

Table 6.6 displays this information by sex for rural Dakshina Kannada.

TABLE 6.6: **Educational Status of Child Workers Who Do Not Attend School**

Sex	*n*	*Educational Status (%)*		
		Never enrolled	*Enrolled but discontinued*	*Total*
Male	45	45.0	55.0	100
Female	64	71.0	29.0	100

Ever-enrolled children in this context refer to those who have passed through atleast first standard in the school. Children whose names were on the roll but were not promoted to the second standard due to any reasons are not considered in this category. Admittedly, in the case of those children, whose educational level was reported as first standard, it was not possible to ascertain whether they were actually promoted to the next class. However, the proportion of children whose educational level was recorded as first standard is not large.

Data displayed in Table 6.6 show that about one-half of full-time male child workers had never got enrolled in a school and another half had to discontinue schooling due to several reasons. A majority of full-time female child workers belong to the former group (71 per cent). Only about 29 per cent of them had passed out of first standard.

Respondents were asked to give reasons for not enrolling in or withdrawing their non-school attending working children from school. Six reasons were reported in all the three villages which are presented in Table 6.7. For boys, in more than 50 per cent of the cases, the help and support the family needed from them was the reason given. In about 27 per cent of the cases, stress was given to the high cost of education. For girls, the convention that girls should not be sent to schools was emphasized in 31 per cent of the cases as the reason which kept them away from schools. Yet, in as high as 26 per cent of the cases, girls were kept away from schools for the help and support the family needed from them. High cost of education was also strongly mentioned as one of the causes of abstaining girls from schools.

Children perform a variety of activities within agriculture and beedi rolling. Mean ages at which they perform these directly productive activities vary by the nature of activities. Children start working by engaging in lighter activities and gradually they pick up activities which require a little skill and more physical exertion.

Sex selectivity of activities performed by children are discernible. Mean ages at which they perform activities also vary by sex. Certain activities girls start performing at a younger age than boys whereas certain other activities boys start doing at a younger age than girls. Table 6.8 shows the participation rate of children in specific activities within agriculture and beedi rolling. Mean age at which these activities are performed and the minimum age at which they start performing these activities are also provided therein.

In Table 6.8, ten activities performed in agriculture by fifty-four male and twenty-seven female children who are working on their family farm are listed. The participation rates of children in these activities indicate that for male children, highest rates are found in animal care and garden cultivation. More than sixty per cent of boys who are engaged in unpaid agricultural activities participate in livestock caring and garden cultivation. About fifty per cent of them engage in weeding. Only a few boys perform or are efficient to perform activities like ploughing and sowing. In other activities like transplanting, manuring, harvesting, picking and peeling, scaring birds, etc. although quite a few boys do engage-in, not more than

TABLE 6.7: **Reasons Given by Parents for Not Enrolling-in or Withdrawing their Children from School**

Reasons	Males		Females	
	Number of cases	*Percentage distribution*	*Number of cases*	*Percentage distribution*
1. Cannot afford school expenses	12	26.7	14	21.5
2. Needed to help and support the family	22	48.9	17	26.2
3. Needed to look after younger siblings	4	8.9	9	13.9
4. Convention does not allow parents to send girls to school	—	—	20	30.8
5. Child is not interested in studies	5	11.1	3	6.2
6. Physically handicapped	2	4.4	1	1.5
N	45		64	

TABLE 6.8: **Participation of Children in Agricultural and Beedi Rolling Activities and their Mean and Youngest Age of Performing these Activities**

Activities	*Males*			*Females*		
	Activity rate	*Mean age of those performing the specific activity*	*Youngest age**	*Activity rate*	*Mean age of those performing in the specific activity*	*Youngest age**
1	*2*	*3*	*4*	*5*	*6*	*7*
Agricultural Activities (N-54 Males, 27 Females)						
1. Ploughing	9.3	13.2	11	0	—	—
2. Sowing	1.9	13.8	12	0	—	—
3. Transplanting	13.0	13.1	11	55.6	13.1	10
4. Manuring	14.8	11.3	8	7.4	15.0	12
5. Weeding	48.2	11.5	8	44.4	13.2	10
6. Harvesting	13.0	11.9	9	44.4	13.5	11
7. Picking and Peeling	14.8	11.6	6	22.2	10.8	6
8. Tending Livestock	66.7	12.1	6	29.6	13.1	7

(*Contd.*)

1	2	3	4	5	6	7
9. Scaring birds	13.0	9.3	6	11.1	10.3	6
10. Garden farming	63.0	11.8	8	22.2	13.5	10
Beedi Rolling Activities (N=50 Males, 60 Females)						
1. Tying beedies	100.0	12.0	10	100.0	10.6	8
2. Closing beedi mouths	100.0	12.0	10	100.0	10.6	8
3. Cutting & shaping beedi leaves	52.0	13.5	12	83.8	13.3	10
4. Beedi making (involving all the activities)	38.0	13.9	12	55.2	13.5	10

*Ages are based on at least 3 cases at that age.

twenty-five per cent of the unpaid agricultural male child workers perform these activities. For girls, high rates of participation are found in transplanting (56 per cent), weeding (44 per cent) and harvesting (44 per cent). Other agricultural activities where female child participation is high are livestock tending (30 per cent), picking and peeling (22 per cent) and garden cultivation (22 per cent).

Weeding is the only activity in agriculture where high rates of participation are found both among boys and girls (48 per cent and 44 per cent, respectively). While in livestock tending and garden cultivation boys dominate over girls in terms of participation rates, high rates of participation by girls than boys are found in activities like transplanting and harvesting. Activities such as ploughing and sowing are, generally, not performed by female children.

Wage earning children are elder ones whose mean age is between 13-14 years. Significant sex-wise differentials in the mean age are not envisaged among these children, but differentials in their earnings are discernible. Male children earn, on an average, nearly six rupees a day whereas female children's average daily earning is not more than four-and-a-half rupees (cash plus imputed value of wage in kind). Sex-wise differentials in the daily earnings of children is owing to the differences in the nature of activities performed by them. Generally, harder work (usually performed by male children) are rewarded more than the lighter work (usually performed by female children). Monthly and annual earnings hinge on the number of days worked by them. Both male and female children earn around ninety-five rupees a month, but the annual earnings of male children in terms of cash and kind is about two hundred rupees more than that of female children. Male and female children earn per annum Rs. 730 and Rs. 540 respectively (See Table 6.9). Male children's earnings account for about 20 per cent of their annual household income. Wage earning female children contribute about 15 per cent of their annual household income.

6.4 Participation in Household Chores

More than one-half of children in school-going age group

TABLE 6.9: **Average Daily, Monthly and Yearly Earnings (Cash and Kind) of Children**

	Daily earnings (Rs.)	*Monthly earnings (Rs.)*	*Yearly earnings (Rs.)*	*Mean age*
Males (N=19)	5.9	95	731	13.7
Females (N=18)	4.5	93	539	13.8

do engage themselves in household duties. Female children participate in larger numbers in these activities than male children and as evident from Table 6.10, their participation rate too is expressively higher. Nearly 70 per cent of boys and 50 per cent of girls performing household duties are recorded as attending school. From among working children, they make up about 45 per cent of total children performing household chores.

Table 6.10 shows that the highest participation of children of both the sexes in household chores is registered in the category of those who combine schooling and work. About 57 per cent of boys and 78 per cent of girls in this category take part in household work. 72 per cent of full-time female child workers also do house work. Higher participation of boys in house work is observed in the category of those who neither work nor go to school as well (39 per cent). Category-wise participation rates presented in the Table suggest that in the category of those who neither work nor go to school, nearly 61 per cent of boys and 43 per cent of girls are absolutely idle and they are economically passive in household production. These children could be potentially harmful to the society.

The work input to household duties in terms of number of days worked per year and hours worked per day show a definite pattern by work-school status of children. Children who neither work nor go to school engage more number of days

TABLE 6.10: **Child Work Intensity in Household Duties by Work-School Status**

	Going to school and not working		*Going to school and also working*		*Working but not going to school*		*Neither working nor going to school*	
	M	*F*	*M*	*F*	*M*	*F*	*M*	*F*
Average number of days worked per year in performing household duties	276	288	212	246	303	327	344	348
Average number of hours spent per day in performing household duties	1.5	2.0	1.4	1.9	1.6	2.5	3.2	3.2
Per cent participation in household duties to the total in the broad category	31.5	55.3	56.8	78.3	28.9	71.9	39.3	56.9
N	34	52	42	36	13	46	22	41

TABLE 6.11: **Participation of Children in Different Household Activities and Their Mean and Youngest Age of Performing these Activities**

Activities	*Males (N=111)*			*Females (N=175)*		
	Activity rate	*Mean age of those performing the specific activity*	*Youngest age**	*Activity rate*	*Mean age of those performing the specific activity*	*Youngest age**
1. Caring for younger siblings	53.2	10.7	6	52.0	10.5	6
2. Helping in household food preparation	9.9	12.9	9	46.3	12.4	9
3. Carrying water for household consumption	66.7	11.7	8	73.7	11.9	8
4. Firewood collection	46.0	11.6	8	36.0	11.9	8
5. Collecting cowdung and preparation of cowdung cakes for household consumption	18.9	11.2	6	20.0	11.5	7

6. Petty shopping for household purposes	42.3	11.3	8	7.4	10.5	8
7. Other household maintenance work (washing clothes, vessels, etc.)	18.0	11.9	7	55.4	11.5	7

*Youngest ages are based on at least 3 cases at that age.

per year and devote more number of hours per day for household duties than their counterparts in the other three categories. In an year, these children engage in household chores for as many as 350 days and they assign about 3.2 hours per day for those activities. Among the other three categories of children, those who work but do not go to school, those who go to school but do not work and those who combine schooling and work stand in that order in terms of intensity of work in household chores. This information by sex is displayed in Table 6.10.

The activity rates of 111 boys and 175 girls who were reported as participating in household chores are presented in Table 6.11. The mean age of children performing these activities and the minimum age at which they start performing these activities are also presented in the Table. In household chores, the highest participation of children of both the sexes is found in carrying water for household consumption (67 per cent of boys and 74 per cent of girls). Other activities in which the participation rate of boys is higher are minding younger siblings (53 per cent), fire-wood collection (46 per cent) and petty shopping (42 per cent). For girls, higher participation is found in household maintenance work (55 per cent), minding younger siblings (52 per cent), helping in household food preparation (46 per cent) and fire-wood collection (36 per cent).

Children start performing various activities involved in housework between 6 to 9 years of age. They start minding the younger ones to free the adults for more productive work when they are six. There is not much variation howsoever either by sex or by activity in the age at which children start discharging household duties. Notwithstanding this, the mean age of children helping in household food preparation is relatively higher for both the sexes. As it is apparent in Table 6.11, the average age of these children remains around thirteen years. The minimum age at which they start helping in this activity is nine years. In contrast, the average age of children performing other activities is less than twelve years for both boys and girls.

7

CAUSES AND CONSEQUENCES OF CHILD WORK PARTICIPATION : FINDINGS FROM THE PRIMARY INVESTIGATION

This chapter presents the descriptive analysis of the relationship between the socio-economic and demographic variables and child work participation and discusses some of the consequences of child work participation on the family. The descriptive analysis of the causes of child work participation shows the magnitude and intensity of child work participation cross-classified by background variables. Chi-square test is used to show the significance and the strength of the relationship between the background variables and the child work participation.

7.1 Causes

In this section the observed variation in the magnitude and intensity of child work participation by household income, land ownership, caste and religion, highest educational level of any member of the household, family size and availability of schooling facility are described. Variations in the magnitude of child work participation by socio-economic groups is studied in terms of the variations in the composition of children of each socio-economic group in the four identified work-school status categories. Proportion of children of each socio-economic group in the above said four categories are taken and the variations in each category by socio-economic groups are looked into. Variations in the intensity of work are studied in terms of the average number of man days worked per annum and the average number of hours worked per day by children in each socio-economic group. The number of man days worked per annum takes care of not only the number of hours worked per day, but also the number of days worked per annum. Hence it appears to be a better index of work intensity.

7.1.1 Household Income and Child Work Participation

As hypothesized, household income and child work participation should show a negative relationship. In other words the highest the income, the lower the child work participation and the lower the income, the higher the child work participation. We have seen in the review of literature and secondary data analysis that the relationship between poverty indicator and child work participation need not be inverse up to some threshold level. Of course, it is not all that easy to figure-out the break-even point and indicate the level from where the inverse relationship between poverty indicator and child work participation starts operating. Moreover, the threshold level may not be the same everywhere and it may vary over a period of time (Rao, *et al.*, 1983: 198).

In our analysis households are divided into three groups according to their annual income. Those with an income of less than Rs. 2,500 per annum constitute the lowest class, Rs. 2,501 to Rs. 4,000 the middle class and those with an income of more than Rs. 4,000 per annum constitute the upper class. Children belonging to each income receipt class are then classified by work-school status for comparison. Annual household income and the work-school status of children are associated and that association is found to be statistically significant for girls as shown in Table 7.1 (first panel).

Looking at the data presented in Table 7.1, one could see that there is no clear pattern in the relationship between household income and children's participation in school and/or work in Dakshina Kannada. However, the negative relationship between the household income and the idleness rate is well pronounced and is as anticipated for both the sexes. An increase in household income brings down the idleness rate

TABLE 7.1: **Percentage Distribution of Children in Each Work-School Status Category by Background Variables**

Background variable	*Work-School Status of Children (6-15)*											
	Children who were attending school but not working		*Children who were attending school and also working*		*Children who were working but not attending school*		*Children who were neither working nor attending school*		*Total*		*Chi-square value between work-school status of children and the background variable*	
	M	*F*	*M*	*F*	*M*	*F*	*M*	*F*	*M*	*F*	*M*	*F*
	1	*2*	*3*	*4*	*5*	*6*	*7*	*8*	*9*	*10*	*11*	*12*
Annual Household Income (Rs.)												
Less than 2500	38.9 (28)	29.0 (20)	19.4 (14)	7.3 (5)	12.6 (9)	26.1 (18)	29.2 (21)	37.7 (26)	100.0 (72)	100.0 (69)		
2501—4000	33.0 (30)	28.3 (26)	29.7 (27)	25.0 (23)	14.3 (13)	18.5 (17)	23.1 (21)	28.3 (26)	100.0 (91)	100.0 (92)	11.96 d.f., 6 not sig. at p. 0.05	19.40 d.f. 6 sig. at p. 0.05
4001 and above	41.7 (50)	41.7 (48)	27.5 (33)	15.7 (18)	19.2 (23)	25.2 (29)	11.7 (14)	17.4 (20)	100.0 (120)	100.0 (115)		
Total	38.2 (108)	34.1 (94)	26.2 (74)	16.7 (46)	15.9 (45)	23.2 (64)	19.8 (56)	26.1 (72)	100.0 (283)	100.0 (276)		

(*Contd.*)

	1	2	3	4	5	6	7	8	9	10	11	12
Operational Land Holding Size												
Landless	39.1 (66)	21.6 (35)	20.1 (34)	12.4 (20)	16.6 (28)	29.6 (48)	24.3 (41)	36.4 (59)	100.0 (169)	100 0 (162)	12.86 d.f. 6 sig. at p. 0.05	48.02 d.f. 6 sig. at p. 0.05
1—2.99 acres	39.0 (23)	50.8 (31)	28.8 (17)	24.6 (15)	17.0 (10)	11.5 (7)	15.3 (9)	13.1 (8)	100.0 (59)	100.0 (61)		
3 acres and above	34.6 (19)	52.8 (28)	41.8 (23)	20.8 (11)	12.7 (7)	17.0 (9)	10.9 (6)	9.4 (5)	100.0 (55)	100.0 (53)		
Total	38.2 (108)	34.1 (94)	26.2 (74)	16.7 (46)	15.9 (45)	23.2 (64)	19.8 (56)	26.1 (72)	100 0 (283)	100.0 (276)		
Number of Siblings (6-15)*												
0—1 sibling	35.3 (59)		18.6 (31)		16.8 (28)		29.3 (49)		100.0 (167)		8.80 d.f. 6 not sig. at p. 0.05	
2 siblings	34.0 (67)		22.8 (45)		19.8 (39)		23.4 (46)		100.0 (197)			
3 and more siblings	39.0 (76)		22.6 (44)		21.5 (42)		16.9 (33)		100.0 (195)			
Total	36.1 (202)		21.5 (120)		19.5 (109)		22.9 (128)		100.0 (559)			

Highest Educational Level of any Adult Member of the Household												
No education	24.8 (26)	22.6 (23)	24.8 (26)	6.9 (7)	18.1 (19)	27.5 (28)	33.0 (34)	43.1 (44)	100.0 (105)	100.0 (102)		
I—IV Std.	44.2 (19)	28.6 (12)	11.6 (5)	21.4 (9)	23.3 (10)	19.1 (8)	20.9 (9)	31.0 (13)	100.0 (43)	100.0 (42)	31.78 d.f. 6	42.14 d.f. 6
V Std. and above	46.7 (63)	44.7 (59)	31.9 (43)	22.7 (30)	11.9 (16)	21.2 (28)	9.6 (13)	11.4 (15)	100.0 (135)	100.0 (132)	sig. at p. 0.05	sig. at p. 0.05
Total	38.2 (108)	34.1 (94)	26.2 (74)	16.7 (46)	15.9 (45)	23.2 (64)	19.8 (56)	26.1 (72)	100.0 (283)	100.0 (276)		
Caste/Religion												
Muslims	39.5 (45)	14.5 (14)	18.4 (21)	10.3 (10)	15.8 (18)	32.0 (31)	26.3 (30)	43.3 (42)	100.0 (114)	100.0 (97)		
Scheduled Castes and Tribes	27.1 (16)	22.2 (10)	27.1 (16)	8.9 (4)	15.3 (9)	35.6 (16)	30.5 (18)	33.3 (15)	100.0 (59)	100.0 (45)	23.40 d.f. 7	70.07 d.f. 7
Middle castes	43.9 (25)	52.4 (33)	29.8 (17)	23.8 (15)	15.8 (9)	11.1 (7)	10.5 (6)	12.7 (8)	100.0 (57)	1000. (63)	sig. at p. 0.05	sig. at p. 0.05
Upper castes	41.5 (22)	52.1 (37)	37.7 (20)	23.9 (17)	17.0 (9)	14.1 (10)	3.8 (2)	9.9 (7)	100.0 (53)	100.0 (71)		
Total	38.2 (108)	34.1 (94)	26.2 (74)	16.7 (46)	15.9 (45)	23.2 (64)	19.8 (56)	26.1 (72)	100.0 (283)	100.0 (276)		

Note: Figures in the parentheses refer to the number of observations.

*Data are not presented separately by sex.

among the children. The drop of idleness rate by 6 per cent points from the lowest class to middle class and by 11 per cent points from middle class to upper class in the case of male children and by 9 per cent points from lower class to middle class and by 11 per cent points from middle class to upper class in the case of female children are apparent in Table 7.1. The pattern becomes clearer for the other three categories of children when we consider only two income receipt classes, *viz.* those with less than Rs. 4,000 and those above Rs. 4,000 per annum. An increase in income boosts up the proportion of full-time school attending children. The percentage of children attending school and not working increases from abount 36 per cent in the case of males and 29 per cent in the case of female in the lower income group to 42 per cent for both the sexes in the higher income group. Richer families can easily afford school expenses—direct and indirect—which result in a larger proportion of full-time school going children. Altogether about 69 per cent male and 57 per cent female children in the sample attend school in the higher income receipt class as against 60 per cent male and 46 per cent female children in the lower income receipt class.

The observed relationship between child work participation and the household income is not inverse. The work participation rate tends to increase with an increase in income as can be seen from Table 7.1. The proportion of boys who work but do not go to school increases remarkably with an increase in income. While about 20 per cent of boys among the households with an annual income of Rs. 4,000 and above participate in full-time work without attending school, the participation rate of boys among households with an annual income of less than Rs. 4.000 is around 14 per cent. In the case of female children the difference is marginal, (*i.e.* about 22 per cent in the lower income group and 25 per cent in the higher income group). Among those who combine schooling and work similar trend is found only in the case of male children.

In the light of the positive relationship between household income and child work participation rate, it can be said that the break-even point for the operation of the inverse relationship between these two variables has not been reached or has been obscured due to lack of some more data on the work participation of children among higher income brackets. Below the break-even point, perhaps the inverse relationship between these two variables is disturbed by other factors like asset ownership, number of adult workers in the family, the number of wage-earning children, etc. Possession of assets like land and live-stock by the 'richer among the poor', provides additional opportunities and encourages participation of their children in work. More number of adult workers in the family in activities like beedi rolling, etc. in spite of improving the household financial condition seek family child labour as helpers. This appears to be the case particularly in Dakshina Kannada district.

There is thus a reciprocal causation between household income and child work participation below the break-even point. To begin with, lower household income induces the households to hire out their children's labour for direct monetary benefits. Thus, lower household income acts as the cause and the child work participation the effect. In many cases children's participation in wage employment improves the financial status of the households and consequently results in asset ownership which in turn encourages further participation of children in work. Ultimately, where it lands up is in a situation with higher income and higher child work participation. In this case, child work participation is the cause and higher household income is the effect. Thus what initially might be an inverse relationship between household income and child work participation ends up in a direct relationship up to a certain level of income. This can be stated as the Paradox of Child Work Participation. Briefly, the paradox of child work participation at household level is presented as follows:

Low Y—→CWP in Wage Employment—→Enhancement in Total Y—→+ve Net Income over Expenditure (savings)—→Purchase of Assets (land, live-stock etc.)—→Increased Opportunities for CWP—→Increase in CWP rate.

The above argument gets empirical support from our sample. It has been found that about 80 per cent of the wage earning children belong to the higher income groups and about

75 per cent of the cultivating land owners have an income of more than Rs. 2,500 per annum.

Households belonging to lower income groups, generally, do not own any assets; this limits the work participation of children within the family. Those who work within the family work by helping the adult members in their tasks. Not all the children in the households with lower income work for wages. Some do not find wage employment and have no family assets to engage in. Those who can manage schooling do so and others remain idle. Even among those who work for wages, some work as casual labourers. Eventually, some of the households belonging to lower income groups remain where they were and the employment of children do not significantly improve their financial conditions.

The nature of the relationship between child work participation rate and the household income can be graphically illustrated. This has been done in Fig. 7.3 which depicts the Backward Bending nature of the child work participation rate curve.

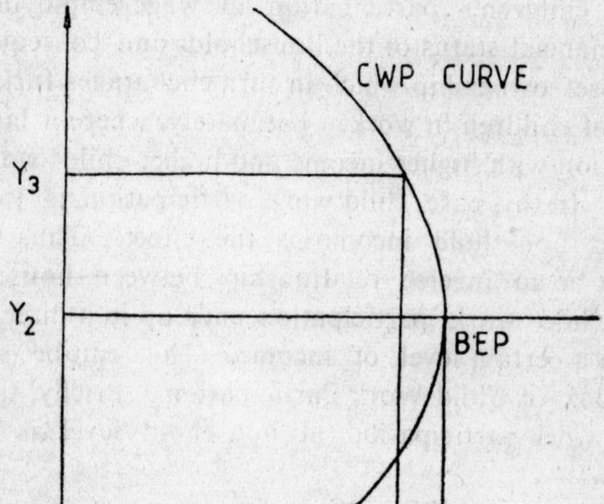

Fig. 7.3 : Backward Bending CWP Curve

The point BEP in the graph is the break-even point corresponding to the income level of OY_2. The increase in income level from OY_1 to OY_2 leads to an increase in OWP rate from OA to OB, thus showing a positive relatiohship. Beyond BEP, the nature of the relationship between CWP rate and Y changes. Above BEP, a rise in income level (from OY_2 to OY_3) brings down the CWP rate from OB to OC indicating the inverse relationship between CWP rate and Y. The change in the nature of the relationship between CWP rate and Y beyond BEP may be due to the status consciousness among the members of the households belonging to higher income groups, effective demand for hired labour, etc.

Now, coming to the intensity of child work participation we have followed the same income groupings for the analysis. Here, working children numbering 214 are classified by their household income and their average annual and daily time input to work is analysed. Table 7.2 (first panel) presents this information.

As in the case of the magnitude of child work participation, Table 7.2 shows a positive association between the household income and the intensity of child work participation both in terms of the average number of man days worked per annum and the average number, of hours worked per day. Once again, this relationship is confined to the area below the break-even point in the graph. Hence the explanation rendered for such a relationship between these two variables follows from the one given for the relationship between the magnitude of child work participation and household income in the earlier paragraphs. What one can understand in the earlier discussion is that working children who belong to the households which remain in the lower income groups are mainly marginal workers in the sense that they either work as helpers to the adult workers in the family or as casual wage labourers. On the other hand, households with higher income have full-time wage-earning child workers. As a result, the average duration of work by children in higher income brackets is found to be higher than that of those in the lower income groups.

TABLE 7.2: **Intensity of Child Work Participation by Background Variables**

Background Variable	*N*	*Average number of hours worked per day*	*Average number of man-days worked per annum*
Annual Household Income (Rs.)			
2500	45	4.5	104
2501 — 4000	81	5.1	125
4001 & above	88	5.5	170
Operated Land Holding Size			
Landless	121	5.9	174
1—2.99 acres	44	4.3	107
3 acres and above	49	3.9	87
Number of Siblings (6—15)			
0 — 1 sibling	56	4.9	146
2 siblings	34	5.0	132
3 and more siblings	74	5.3	148
Highest Educational Level of any Adult Member of the Household			
No education	77	5.8	147
I — IV Standard	36	6.0 } 4.7	192 } 138
V standard and above	101	4.3 }	118 }
Caste/Religion			
Muslims	72	5.5	179
Scheduled Castes and Scheduled Tribes	46	6.0	129
Middle Castes	46	4.3	132
Upper Castes	50	3.9	104

7.1.2 Land Ownership and Child Work Participation

Size of operated land holding has been taken as an indicator of the economic status of the household. But the question whether it provides a true indication of economic status leads us to suspect the validity of the indicator, especially in the present study under different reasoning. First, in the sample, about 50 per cent of the households are landless and hence definitely are deriving the major portion of their household income from non-farm activities and wage labour. A large proportion of those who own land are marginal land owners. Rest are small and medium land owners. Secondly though the households derive some income from farm, it is reasonable to think that the major portion of their income need not come from agriculture. Moreover agricultural yield depends upon the quality of land, irrigation and variety of other factors. Therefore it appears that land ownership is not a good indicator of the economic status or the disposable income of the household. However, we have made an attempt to analyse the variations in child work participation by operated land holding size.

For purpose of analysis, three land ownership categories are made, *viz.* landless, marginal and owners (1 to 2.99 acres) and small (3 to 4.99 acres) and medium land owners (5 to 9.99 acres). Large land owners (10 acres and above) in our sample, are totally absent. One-half of children aged 6-15 years in the sample belong to landless households. The rest belong to the marginal, small and medium land ownership class. The classification of work-school status of children by operated land ownership class are provided in Table 7.1 (second panel). The association between these two variables is found to be statistically significant for both boys and girls.

In Table 7.1, idleness rate of children is found to be the highest among the landless households (24 per cent among boys and 36 per cent among girls) and it drops sharply as the household possesses more and more cultivable land. Thus land ownership seems to encourage child work participation and/or schooling. Table 7.1 shows that, within landowning classes, possession of more land improves the schooling rate and increases the work participation rate of boys whereas it does not exercise significant influence on the participation (both school and work) of girls. The schooling rate of boys improves from 68 per cent among marginal land owning class to 76 per cent among small and medium land owners. The increase in work participation rate is from 46 per cent to 55 per cent.

When we compare the participation rates of children of the landless and the land-owning class, a clear pattern emerges in the schooling and work participation rate for both the sexes. The schooling rate shows an improvement from 59 per cent to 72 per cent for boys and from just 34 per cent to above 70 per cent for girls. This supports the common belief that the better off families can well afford and their attitudes are inclined to send their children to school. Also, our data support the argument that land ownership taps potential family labour and encourages children to participate in labour force very early in their life. Though the rate of participation of girls in work does not increase by possession of land, that of boys shows a steep rise from about 37 per cent among the landless to 50 per cent among the land owning class. Thus, the possession of land facilitates children to combine schooling and work. The proportion of those who combine schooling and work shows a definite increase with the possession of land. The proportion of boys combining schooling and work rises from about 20 per cent among landless to 35 per cent among the land owning class. The corresponding increase for girls in this category is from about 12 per cent to 22 per cent. It should be noted that possession of land draws more boys to work than girls and on the other hand, the improvement in the economic status of the household as indicated by the land-ownership has a better impact on the schooling rate of girls than that of boys.

This finding is similar to that of Vlassoff's observation in rural Maharashtra as far as the impact of land acquisition on child work participation (Vlassoff, 1979: 424) is concerned. But the difference to be noted between Vlassoff's and this study is that when we study the variations in the actual child work participation rates by land ownership class, he constructed a work index for children where parents were asked to say whether the economic activities children performed were of much help, some help or no help. Inherently the answers would be subjective. Moreover, Vlassoff did not classify the households by landownership. Instead his conclusion is based on the variations observed by standard of living where land was one of the elements of standard of living index. However, Nadkarni's (Nadkarni, 1976: 1165) analysis based on data from Maharashtra is similar to the one carried out in this study. Of course, the findings of this study contradicts Nadkarni's observation in Maharashtra. But no comparison of the findings of the two studies is ventured in this regard, especially, because the mode of classification of the land-holding is entirely different.

Though land ownership results in higher child work participation rates, the intensity of child work participation need not be very high. In fact, the average number of hours worked per day and the man days worked per annum by children cross-classified by land ownership (Table 7.2, second panel) shows a negative relationship between these two variables in rural Dakshina Kannada. Before explaining the observed nature of the relationship, it should be remembered that the working children of landless households are not engaged in farm activities within the family and hence are either engaged in non-farm activities carried out by the family (beedi rolling, etc.) or in wage labour. The difference in the proportion of full-time workers by the acquisition of more land, on the other hand, is not all that significant and hence the intensity of work by children slackens with the possession or more land.*

7.1.3 Sibling Number and Child Work Participation

We assume that, given the limited resources, the higher the number of children in the family, the lower is the average time-input to work. But Nag *et al.*, (Nag *et al.*, 1978: 297), in their study observed the contrary. They observed that the children with more number of siblings put-in more time to work (including household duties) than the children with less number of siblings or no siblings at all. One of the reasons suspected

*The work intensity of those children who combine schooling and work is comparatively lower.

by them suggest that children in large families are encouraged by the presence of elder siblings to participate in work and to begin work at an early age. If this is true, the work participation rate among children with more number of siblings should be higher than the rate among the children with less number of siblings or no siblings at all. Even our hypothesis shows a direct relationship between these two variables although our reasoning is different. We hypothesized that, given the financial constraints, parents are forced to send some of their children to work to keep them away from idleness, for, the available resources do not allow them to send all their children to school. In the light of the data presented in Table 7.1 (third panel). Nag *et al's.*, argument seems to be more acceptable and more reasonable. However, they did not explicitly distinguish between magnitude and intensity of child work participation. Though their argument appears to be applicable to the direct relationship between the number of siblings and the child work participation rate, the information provided by them show the direct relationship between the number of siblings and the intensity of child work participation. Moreover, their argument is based on the work-input of children in all the activities (including household work). In the present analysis, the effect of number of siblings on the magnitude and intensity of child work participation are studied separately.

Table 7.1 (third panel) presents the schooling, work participation and the idleness rates of children by sibling (6-15 years) number. The rates are computed for three groups of children, *viz.* those with one sibling or none, with two siblings and with three or more siblings. Results show that the highest work participation rate is among those who have three or more siblings (45 per cent) followed by those with two siblings (43 per cent) and with one sibling or none (35 per cent). Schooling rate also shows a similar pattern. The highest schooling rate is found among those with three or more siblings (62 per cent), next highest among those within two siblings (57 per cent) and the lowest rate is among those with one sibling or none. It appears that the reason suspected by Nag *et al.*, for the pattern of higher work participation of children in larger families and the lower work participation of children in smaller families holds good with regard to schooling rate as well. If the above pattern of work participation and schooling rates are due to 'encouragement' factor, then the idleness rate in larger families should be much lower than what it is in smaller families. Data in Table 7.1 however, show the assumed pattern of the idleness rate. The highest idleness rate is detected among those children with one or no sibling (29 per cent), than among those with two siblings (23 per cent), and the lowest idleness rate is found among those with three or more siblings (17 per cent). Based on this information one would accept Nag *et al's.*, hypothesis that participation of elder siblings encourages the younger siblings to follow suit. Nevertheless, the Chi-square value obtained shows that the association between the work-school status of children and the number of siblings they have got is not significant in statistical terms.

Work intensity of children and number of siblings seem to have a positive association in rural Dakshina Kannada (Table 7.2, third panel). With due note that, in the present analysis the components of work intensity excludes the time spent for household duties, the similarity of the results obtained in the present investigation with that of Nag *et al.*, study in Java and Nepal is worth-mentioning. Again, it may be the 'encouragement' factor which is operating. On the other hand, there is no significant direct variation in the proportion of subsidiary child workers with the number of siblings. Full-time workers include those who are working on their own farm, at home, and for wages. Comparatively they put-in more time to work than the subsidiary workers. Thus, more time input to work by children with larger number of siblings compared to those with smaller number of siblings is self-explanatory.

7.1.4 Educational Level and Child Work Participation

As hypothesized, the educational level of the members of the family affect the child work participation. The nature of this relationship is expected to be negative. The highest educational level of any adult member of the family is the proxy used in this analysis to study the influence of the educational achievement of the decision-maker on child work participation.

It has been assumed here that educated adult members in the family will be having a say over the decision of the head of the household regarding children's schooling or work. The main reason for not taking straight-away the educational level of the head of the household (decision-maker) as the indicator is due to the fact that a large proportion of them are illiterate. Rest of them are semi-literate or just literate with a couple of years of schooling. Percentage of the heads of households with educational level of more than primary school is negligible. It has been anticipated that variations in child work participation will not be distinguishable between households with illiterate, semi-literate or just literate heads of households.

Three educational groupings are made for the present study, *viz* households whose highest educational level of any member is (i) no education, (ii) primary schooling (I-IV standard, and (iii) middle schooling and above (V and above). Out of 559 children in our analysis 37 per cent belong to households with no literate adult member. Another 15 per cent children belong to those households whose highest educational level of any adult member is primary level. Remaining 48 per cent children have in their family at least an adult member with an educational level of Standard V and above. The observed difference in the work-school status of children by these educational groups is statistically significant for both boys and girls.

The association of the highest educational level of any adult member of the household with the rate of exclusive participation of children in school *vis-a-vis* the idleness rate is well marked for both the sexes. The relationshiy with the former is direct and with the latter it is inverse. The overall schooling rates of boys and girls also give positive relationship with the educational variable of the household. But the variation in the child work participation by the variation in the independent variable under consideration is not apparent. This information is presented in Table 7.1 (fourth panel).

One anticipates higher child work participation rate with illiteracy prevailing among the adult members in the households and lower child work participation with highest levels of education among the adult members. But data presented in

Table 7.1 do not reveal a clear picture of the anticipated nature of the relationship. Even when we consider separately those child workers who combine schooling with work and those who do not, the expected nature of the relationship does not emerge with clarity. However, when we consider only two groups of households in the sample, viz. one consisting of those who do not have any educated adult person and the other consisting of those households having atleast one educated adult member, the deterring impact of educational level on child work participation rate becomes obvious in the case of male children. The work participation rate of boys comes down from about 43 per cent in the illiterate group to 41 per cent in the literate group. Though the fall in the work participation rate is not significant, the declining trend is noted. In the case of female child workers the expected trend is still not observed.

From the above analysis, one can argue that the educational level of the adult members of the household has a better impact on the schooling rate of children than on the child work participation rate. Besides it exerts a tremendous downward influence on the idleness rate. Higher schooling rate by the presence of educated persons in the household draws children away as much from the work force as it is from the idle group. While there is a 29 per cent point improvement in the schooling rate of boys and a 38 per cent point improvement in that of girls from the lowest educational group to the highest educational group, a large percentage of this increase (80 per cent for boys and 84 per cent for girls) is seemingly explained by the decline in the idleness rate.

Though not the work participation rate, the educational level of the adult members in the household may significantly influence the duration of work of children. Table 7.2 (fourth panel) provides data on the work intensity of children by educational level of the adult members in the household. The Table shows a clear trend with high work intensity of children among the illiterate group and low work intensity among the literate group. Thus one can infer that educational levels of adult members in the household starts exercising its influence on the child work participation by reducing the duration of work performed by children.

7.1.5 Caste Religion and Child Work Participation

Caste is assumed to be an important factor influencing child work participation in India. It determines the economic status of the family, family size and the educational status of the household. In the present sample, out of 285 households 188 belong to Hindus (66 per cent) and the remaining 97 (34 per cent) belong to Muslims. Since Muslims constitute a significant proportion in the sample, a comparison of child work participation between Muslims and Hindus is possible in this analysis. Among Hindu households, 33 per cent belong to Scheduled Castes and Scheduled Tribes, another 33 per cent belong to Middle caste group and the remaining 34 per cent households belong to upper castes. The upper caste Hindus include Brahmins and Bunts whereas middle caste group comprises of Pujaris, Acharis, Devadigas, Moilies, etc. The observed association between caste/religion and the work-school status of children is statistically significant for both the sexes.

Caste/religion influences child work participation not directly but through intervening variables which are economic, demographic and educational. This necessitates a knowledge of economic, demographic and educational characteristics of the households belonging to various caste/religion groups. These are given in Table 7.3. As per the Table upper caste

TABLE 7.3: **Economic, Demographic and Educational Characteristics of Households by Caste/Religion**

Caste/Religion	*Average annual income per house-hold (Rs.)*	*Average size of land holding (acres)*	*Average size of the household*	*Per cent household with at least a literate member*
Muslims	3978	0.70	8.4	56.7
Scheduled Castes and Scheduled Tribes	2768	2.19	5.8	27.4
Middle Caste	4498	1.85	6.3	73.8
Upper Caste	5013	3.22	7.5	90.8

Hindus are economically the most advantaged section in the society both in terms of annual income and in terms of land ownership. This has a reflection on their educational status. About 91 per cent of the households belonging to the upper castes has atleast one literate adult member in the family. The corresponding figures for middle castes, scheduled groups and Muslims are 74 per cent, 27 per cent and 57 per cent respectively. In terms of annual income, middle caste households stand as second highest in the sample followed by Muslims and Scheduled Castes and Tribes. The land ownership pattern shows that Muslims are generally landless. The major source of their income is from non-farm activities such as trading, business, beedi rolling, etc. The average size of land-holding of the middlc castes and the Scheduled Castes and Tribes do not vary much in the sample. A better land ownership position of the Scheduled Castes and Tribes could be due to the recent land redistribution policies of the government.

Data presented in the Table show that the social groups have distinct demographic characteristics. The size of the household is found to be the largest among Muslims and Brahmins among Hindus. Scheduled Caste and Tribe households in the sample are characterised by the smaller size of their household. Large household size among Muslims may be due to the high fertility prevailing among them whereas among upper caste Hindus the still existing joint-family system may be the major reason. Information collected from the field reveal that Scheduled Castes and Scheduled Tribes prefer nuclear family in view of the benefits they receive from the government. This may be the reason for the smaller size of households among the Scheduled groups.

Based on our analyses presented in the previous sections of this chapter one can envisage higher schooling rate, higher work participation rate and a very low idleness rate among the children of the upper caste mainly because of the fact that they are the land-owning group in the society. According to the data presented in Table 7.1 (fifth panel) it is so with respect to schooling rate and idleness rate and partially so with respect to work participation rate. The schooling rate is the highest among the upper caste group for both the sexes. The schooling rate of boys among them is 79 per cent whereas among middle castes, Scheduled Castes and Scheduled Tribes and Muslims, it is 74 per cent, 54 per cent and 58 per cent respectively. The schooling rate for girls is 76 per cent among upper caste and middle caste, 31 per cent among Scheduled Castes and Scheduled Tribes and 25 per cent among Muslims. Low schooling rates of both the sexes among the unprivileged castes (Scheduled Castes and Scheduled Tribes) can be clearly noticed from the data. The schooling rate of boys is the lowest among this caste group and that of girls is found to be the lowest among the Muslims. The religious prejudices against sending girls to school prevalent among the Muslims could be the cause for the lowest schooling rate of girls among them. Between Hindus and Muslims, the former have higher schooling rate than the latter for both the sexes. It has been observed that a large number of Muslim children attend religious classes to learn Koran and Arabic at the cost of formal schooling.

The overall work participation rates by caste/religion show different patterns for boys and girls. The highest work participation rate for boys is found among Hindus (47 per cent) than among Muslims (34 per cent). Within Hindus, it is the participation rate of boys belonging to the upper castes which is higher compared to those belonging to the lower castes. With regard to female children, higher work participation rate is found among Muslims (42 per cent) than among Hindus (39 per cent) and within Hindus, among Scheduled Castes and Tribes (44 per cent) than among upper castes (37 per cent). Probably, the work participation rates are determined more by economic factors than by sociological or educational factors. It could be noticed that higher work participation rates of boys are among those caste/religion groups whose land-ownership position is relatively better. It is the work participation rates of those boys who attend school which makes all the difference in the overall work participation rates by caste/religion.* On the basis of these two observations,

---

*The work participation rates of boys who do not attend school are almost the same by caste/religion.

we conclude that it is the land ownership pattern which resulted in higher work participation rates of boys among upper castes compared to lower castes and among Hindus compared to Muslims. With regard to female children, however, the expected higher work participation rate among Scheduled Castes and Scheduled Tribes was observed. But comparatively higher participation of girls in work among Muslims than among Hindus was not anticipated. This may be because of the low schooling rate among them and the predominance of beedi-rolling industry in the Muslim dominated area of the study. Beedi-rolling activity does not compel them to go out of their houses and hence they need not break their religious sanction by participating in work. Otherwise, possibly the work participation rate of Muslim girls would have been very low. In fact, more than 90 per cent of Muslim girls participating in work are beedi rollers. When we consider the participation of children in wage employment, the highest percentage of boys is found among Scheduled Castes and Scheduled Tribes (58 per cent) and among Muslims (36 per cent). The percentage of girls in wage employment is found to be the highest among Scheduled Castes and Scheduled Tribes (69 per cent) followed by middle castes (24 per cent).

Idleness rate has a clear pattern by caste/religion in rural Dakshina Kannada. One can expect more number of idle children among Muslims and Scheduled Castes and Scheduled Tribes whose schooling rates are comparatively lower. The expected pattern emerges for both the sexes with very high idleness rates among Muslims (26 per cent for boys and 43 per cent for girls) and Scheduled Castes and Scheduled Tribes (31 per cent for boys and 33 per cent for girls) and low rates among upper castes (4 per cent for boys and 10 per cent for girls) and middle castes (11 per cent for boys and 13 per cent for girls).

So far we were discussing about the association between caste/religion and child work participation rate. Now to analyse the caste influence on the intensity of child work participation, we shall turn our attention to Table 7.2 (fifth panel). The Table indicates that Muslim children put in more time to work than Hindu children. Among the Hindus, it is the Scheduled Caste and Scheduled Tribe children and the middle caste children who spend more time for work than the upper caste children. In terms of the average number of hours worked per day, Scheduled Caste and Scheduled Tribe children worked for a longer time than the Muslim children or children belonging to the middle or upper caste. While Scheduled Caste and Scheduled Tribe children worked for about six hours on normal days, Muslim children worked for 5.5 hours, middle caste children for just above four hours and upper caste children for less than four hours. Higher work-input per day by Scheduled Caste and Scheduled Tribe children and Muslim children may be due to their higher participation in wage employment.

7.1.6 Schooling Facility and Child Work Participation

The association between schooling facility and child work participation, in this study, is not analysed at the household level but at the village level. The three villages selected for the study, *viz.* Ajjavara, Munnur and Neriya are listed in that order on the basis of schooling facilities available. As mentioned in Chapter 5, the presence of and/or the distance to the high school has been taken as the criterion to classify them by schooling facilities. To repeat what we have said in Chapter 5, Ajjavara has got a high school in the village, Munnur though does not have a high school has the nearest high school not very far from the village, with frequent bus transport convenience and in Neriya children are deprived of a high school, the nearest high school being secluded from the village by about 14 kilometres without proper transport facility.

Child work participation rate was expected to be high in Neriya where children are forced to drop-out from school once they complete their primary schooling due to the absence of a high school facility in the village. High cost (direct, indirect and opportunity cost) of high school education make schooling beyond primary education possible only for the better off families. When asked about the reasons for the school drop-out in spite of successful completing primary education, a significant proportion of the respondents expressed their inability to finance their children's stay outside the village so as to provide them high school education. In Munnur and Ajjavara this problem is not encountered due to the proximity to the high school.

Children who drop-out from schools may join the work force. If it is true, then the work participation rate in the village without a high school may be higher than the work participation rate in the village with a high school. However, the observed work participation rates for boys show the highest participation rate in Neriya (61 per cent) and the lowest in Ajjavara (21 per cent). In Munnur about 44 per cent work participation is observed among boys. The village-wise pattern of work participation rates among boys thus observed may be partially due to the varying distance to the nearest high school. A similar pattern of village-wise work participation rates would have been observed for female children also but for the highest work participation rate for girls in Munnur (54 per cent). It has to be borne in mind that Munnur is a Muslim dominated village and hence the proximity to the school may not have much impact on the participation of girls. However, the participation rate of girls in work is found to be higher in Neriya (41 per cent) than in Ajjavara (18 per cent).

7.2 Consequences of Child Work Participation

In this section some of the consequences of child work participation are presented. First, the consequences of child work participation on the child are elaborated and this is followed by a description of the impact of child work participation mainly on the family.

As explained in Chapter 3, child work participation may adversely affect child's attendance or performance in school and its physical or psychological development. Though it was not possible to collect data on school attendance and performance of children in the sample (working and non-working) due to identification problem, school level information pertaining to the attendance of children at different points of time in a year and the general performance of children in school examinations were collected. This has been compared village-wise. It was expected that in Neriya and Munnur where the proportion of children combining schooling and work is relatively higher, the attendance in the school will be lower which may result in the poor performance of children in examinations. In Ajjavara both school attendance and performance were expected to be better since their proportion is lower. The expected variation was, however, not observed with regard to attendance. School attendance in Neriya and Munnur was more or less similar to that found in Ajjavara in all the classes. The impact of child work participation on school attendance is, thus, not explained by the data collected. However, difference in the overall school performance of children belonging to the three villages is noticed. The performance of children studying in schools located in Munnur is recorded to be poorer (less than 60 per cent promotion in all the classes) than of those studying in schools located in Neriya or Ajjavara (more than 70 per cent promotion in all the classes). If the difference in school performance of children belonging to Munnur and Ajjavara is partially due to work participation of school-going children, then the school performance of children belonging to Neriya also should have been poorer compared to those belonging to Ajjavara. But that is not so. This may be attributed to the difference in the mode of compatibility of schooling and work observed in these two villages. Children combining schooling and work in Munnur are mostly employed in beedi-rolling activities whereas in Neriya, they are largely engaged in agricultural activities. In Neriya, children who combine schooling and work, do so during school vacations whereas in Munnur beedi rolling children besides working during school vacations engage in that activity after school hours. This may be directly hindering their studies to result in poor performance in the school. While collecting data from the school, headmasters were asked to give an account of the attendance and performance of children in general. In Munnur, headmasters of both the Government Higher/Primary schools reported that children who fared very badly in the examinations were those who rolled beedies at home. They were reported to be regular to school but were often late. Frequency of late arrivals of students to the schools located in Ajjavara and Neriya is reported to be very less.

It is not possible, in this study, to provide evidence for answering how the work participation of children retards their physical and psychological development. In fact, no attempt was made to collect information on this aspect because that itself becomes a separate research theme. However, during the stay in the village beedi-rolling children were found to be less socialised and lacking recreation. Also, poor performance in the school by these children indicates their slow development.

Child work participation may result in additional income to the household. This is particularly so when there are wage-earning children in the family. Child's contribution to the household income may be direct in terms of cash/kind or may be indirect in terms of production. Those children who work for wages, most of the time, give their earnings wholly or partially to their parents (head of the household), thus contributing directly to the family income. Other category of children who work on the family farm, in family business or in household industry add to the total production in the household economy and hence indirectly contribute to the household income.

Table 7.4 shows that more than 55 per cent of the wage-earning children in the sample contribute very significantly to their household income in terms of cash. While about 32 per cent of them contribute more than 25 per cent of their annual

TABLE 7.4: **Annual Contribution of Wage Earning Children to Their Family Income**

Annual contribution (cash) in terms of percentage to the household income	*N*	*Percentage distribution*
Less than 10%	17	44.7
10%—25%	9	23.7
25% and above	12	31.6
Total	38	100.0

household income, remaining 24 per cent children's contribution accounts for 10 to 25 per cent. The point to be highlighted here is the excessive dependence of the families to which these children belong upon the earnings of children. Then, is it not the economic reason which forced these families to let their children enter the labour market for an economic contribution? It appears to be so. Probably, when we ask this question directly to the members of these families they may admit it. But, there is a large proportion of households wherein children's contribution to the household income is indirect. Those who benefit from their work contribution do not realize it especially due to the nature of the activities they perform. In Munnur, children who help the adults by tying the rolled beedies, or by cutting the leaves for beedi-making in a way are adding to the total beedi production of the household, thereby contributing to the household income. By working on the family farm, they may be sharing the work-input of the adults which otherwise would have reduced their leisure time. At home definitely they are useful to the adult females for looking after younger ones and for performing other time-consuming activities as it was observed especially in the Scheduled Caste households in Ajjavara. Incidentally, the women's work participation among these households is also found to be comparatively higher. One may, therefore, conclude that children who perform household chores and other menial time-consuming activities free adults, especially women, from these activities to perform more productive and important tasks.

Children working for wages in Dakshina Kannada put in almost as much time (daily input) to work as by the adults. On the family farm a full-time child workers' time-input to work makes up one-third to two-thirds of an adult member's duration of work. In the beedi-rolling industry a full-time beedi-rolling child, like an adult rolls beedies for about eight hours a day. Those who combine schooling and work put in around one-third of an adult member's time-input to work both for family farm activities and for beedi-rolling activities. Thus, the information regarding the time-input to work also chimes that the child work-input is significant to the household production.

Assuming the low cost of bearing and rearing children in rural areas, it has been argued that a large family with more number of children is prefered to a small family with less number of children due to the significant economic contribution of children in terms of money or work. This leads us to presume that given all other determinants of fertility, higher economic contribution of children to the family in a particular area should, for this area, show higher fertility rate and the lower economic contribution of children should show a lower fertility rate. To test this hypothesis we do not have any data to indicate fertility levels. However, from the available data we have used the child-woman ratio as the fertility indicator.

The unit of analysis to show the consequence of the economic contribution of children on the fertility levels is the village. Neriya and Munnur where the child work participation of children is higher are expected to have higher child-woman ratios compared to Ajjavara. Data show that it is so with the highest child-woman ratio of 698 in Munnur, followed by 605 in Neriya and 566 in Ajjavara. High child-woman ratio in Munnur may also be due to the concentration of Muslims in that village. Absence of household level analysis, in this study, to understand the impact of economic contribution of children on the parents' desire for children make us reluctant to draw any conclusion on this aspect. All that we can show is the indication of higher levels of fertility in the areas with higher child work participation.

Finally, the impact of child work participation on the adult employment situation in the society and on the overall wage rate are untouched aspects in this study. Yet, it should be noted that adults found it difficult in Neriya to get into the estate work (especially during coffee seeds plucking seasons) due to the preference shown for children to adults for that job. It has been reported that children are paid only Rs. 4 per day, whereas adults doing the same quantum of work have to be paid Rs. 7.

8

PERCEPTIONS OF CHILD WORK PARTICIPATION AND OLD-AGE SECURITY

In the previous chapter the realization of the work and income utility of children by background variables was presented. The present chapter is devoted to highlight how the parents, perceive work utility of children. An attempt is also being made to understand their attitudes towards sending their children to school. We have also shown how much of the perceived old-age security utility of children is being realized.

8.1 Work Utility of Children as Mothers Perceive It

A series of structured questions were asked to mothers and prospective mothers (females aged 20-45 years) in order to know their perceptions of work utility of children and their attitudes towards sending children to school. This information is relevant to compare the realization of work utility of children by parents with their perceptions. Of course, our information regarding perception is limited only to 211 female respondents in the age group of 20-45 years. The questions on attitudes started by asking the eligible females to give their opinion about the least amount of education that a child needs now-a days to make (what they consider) a satisfactory living. The answers which are classified into six categories are presented in Table 8.1. As the Table indicates a large proportion of respondents feel that now-a-days boys need a minimum of VIII to X standard and girls V-VII standard of education. Relatively large number of respondents expressed the need for higher education for boys than for girls. The difference in the responses given on male and female children become more clear in Table 8.2. It shows that 57 per cent of the respondents suggested same level of education for both male and female children. Remaining 43 per cent of them mentioned different levels of education as the minimum needed.

Respondents were asked whether they are planning to send any of their sons or daughters (sons/daughters they might have) to school up to SSLC or above. About 56 per cent of the responses for girls and 33 per cent of the responses for boys were negative (See Table 8.3). Table 8.4 shows the similarities and the differences in the responses given for male and female children. Nearly 33 per cent of the total respondents gave negative responses affirmatively for males and females. 18 per cent of them answered affirmatively for male and negatively for females. As hypothesised no respondent was planning to send her daughter to school by depriving her son of the same benefit.

TABLE 8.1: **Minimum Education that a Child Needs Now-a-days to Make a Satisfactory Living**

Responses	*Male child*		*Female child*	
	No. of cases	*Per cent*	*No. of cases*	*Per cent*
No Education needed	1	0.5	11	5.2
I—IV standard	17	8.1	56	26.5
V—VII standard	56	26.5	85	40.3
VIII—X standard	98	46.4	39	18.6
Above X standard	28	13.3	10	4.7
Cannot say	11	5.2	10	4.7
N	211		211	

Test of goodness of fit significant at both 0.05 and 0.01 levels (Between the minimum education needed for boys and girls). Observed frequencies for boys are taken as expected frequencies for girls.

TABLE 8.2: **Minimum Education that a Child Needs Now-a-days to Make a Satisfactory Living—Male and Female Cross-Classified**

	Male Child				
	I-IV std.	*V-VII std.*	*VIII-X std.*	*Above X std.*	*Total*
Female Child					
I—IV Std.	18 (9.0)	18 (9.0)	22 (11.0)	0 (0.0)	58
V—VII Std.	0 (0.0)	27 (13.5)	25 (12.5)	9 (4.5)	61
VIII—X Std.	0 (0.0)	0 (0.0)	59 (29.5)	12 (6.0)	71
Above X Std.	0 (0.0)	0 (0.0)	0 (0.0)	10 (5.0)	10
Total	18	45	106	31	200

Note : Figures in the parentheses refer to per cent responses.

TABLE 8.3: **Attitude Towards Sending any of Their Children (they might have) to School Up to X Standard or Above**

	Male child		*Female child*	
	No. of cases	*Per cent*	*No. of cases*	*Per cent*
Yes	82	38.9	33	15.7
No	69	32.7	118	55.9
Depends	60	28.4	60	28.4
Total	211	100.0	211	100.0

TABLE 8.4: **Attitude Towards Sending any of Their Children (they might have) to School Up to X Standard or Above—Male and Female Cross-Classified**

	Male child			
	Yes	*No*	*Depends*	*Total*
Female Child				
Yes	26 (12.3)	0 (0.0)	4 (1.9)	30
No	37 (17.5)	69 (32.7)	14 (6.6)	120
Depends	13 (6.2)	7 (3.3)	41 (19.4)	61
Total	76	76	59	211

Note: Figures in the parentheses refer to per cent responses.

Respondents who responded negatively to the above question, were asked to list out the reasons for the same. The reasons given are classified into five categories and they are presented in Table 8.5 for both the sexes. In several cases more than one reason was given. Results from Table 8.5 indicate that parents are conscious about school expenses which is reported as very high in their opinion. Expenses incurred in sending children for higher level of education appears to be the main factor discouraging parents to plan for their children's higher education. The responses given for male and female children do not vary significantly except for the fact that relatively larger proportion of respondents gave reasons coming under 'others' category for female children. The reasons incorporated under the title 'others' include (i) the social norm that females should not be sent for higher education even if they are very intelligent; (ii) school distance; (iii) physical handicap, etc. However, a significantly large per cent of respondents mentioned, for both the sexes, the work and support they expect from their children as the reason they deprive their children of higher education.

TABLE 8.5: **Reasons Given for Not Sending Children to School (up to X standard or above)**

Responses	*Male child* No. of cases	(N=69) Per cent response	*Female child* No. of cases	(N=118) Per cent response
School expenses are too high for their family	57	82.6	60	50.9
Children are needed for work, cannot go to school for that reason	19	27.5	31	26.3
Children must supplement family income, cannot go to school for that reason	7	10.2	8	6.8
Other reasons given	4	5.8	50	42.4
No reason given or reason not clear	2	2.9	3	2.5

All the respondents were then asked to give the age at which children would begin to make a useful contribution. The responses given were put into four categories, *viz.* (i) 8 years and less, (ii) 9-11 years, (iii) 12 years and above, and (iv) no help expected. Table 8.6 which presents this information by sex indicates that children generally begin to work before they cross their eighth year of life. Nearly 50 per cent of responses for boys and 62 per cent of responses for girls uphold the above opinion. The responses indicating 'no help expected' were very small in number for both the sexes. The difference in the age at which boys and girls start making an useful contribution is incisive. As is explicit in Table 8.7, 75 per cent of the respondents gave the same age for both the sexes, out of which 48 per cent, mentioned 8 years and less as the age at which children of both the sexes begin to be economically active.

TABLE 8.6: **Age at Which Children Begin to Work**

Responses	*Male Child*		*Female child*	
	No. of cases	*Per cent*	*No. of cases*	*Per cent*
8 years and less	103	48.8	130	61.6
9—11 years	58	27.5	55	26.1
12 years and above	48	22.8	24	11.4
No help expected	2	0.9	2	0.9
Total	211	100.0	211	100.0

Test of goodness of fit significant at both 0.05 and 0.01 levels (Between the age at which boys and girls should begin to work). Observed frequencies for males are taken as expected frequencies for females.

TABLE 8.7: **Age at Which Children Begin to Work—Male and Female Cross-Classified**

	8 years and below	*9-11 years*	*12 years & above*	*Total*
	Male Child			
Female Child				
8 years and below	101 (48.3)	27 (12.9)	4 (1.9)	132
9-11 years	2 (1.0)	31 (14.8)	20 (9.6)	53
12 years and above	0 (0.0)	0 (0.0)	24 (11.5)	24
Total	103	58	48	209

Note : Figures in the parentheses refer to per cent responses.

Only 1 per cent mentioned higher ages for girls and lower ages for boys whereas about 24 per cent of the respondents gave lower age for girls and higher ages for boys, with an implication that girls, generally, become economically active at a younger age than boys.

Finally, respondents who had atleast one child in the 6-15 group were asked to say how important they felt is the participation of their child/children in activities at home, on the family farm, in the family business, etc. The respondents numbering 192 were given three choices, *viz*. much help, some help and no help. About 7 per cent of the respondents did not make any comments. Among the rest about 23 per cent attached no importance to the activities children performed. But a majority of respondents perceived some help in the activities children performed at home and outside home. For 18 per cent of the respondents, children were of much help to them (See Table 8.8).

TABLE 8.8: **Women's Perception of Help from Children**

Responses	*No. of cases (N=211)*	*Per cent response*
Much help	38	18.0
Some help	110	52.3
No help	49	23.2
Cannot say	14	6.6

8.2 Children as Old-Age Security

This section brings out how children are perceived as old-age security and how much of this security utility of children has been realised. Perceptions are those of females of 20-45 years and the realisations those of the aged.

Females of 20-45 years (numbering 211) were asked to reflect on the financial support they expect when they and their husbands can no longer work. It was found that a majority of respondents (80 per cent) referred to children as the major source of financial support in old age. Respondents were also asked whether they expect to live with their children when their children are grown up and married. About 85 per cent of the responses were in the affirmative. Most of the women who expected to live with their children in future expected to be with them for the rest of their life (74 per cent).

Information from this study relating to parents' perceptions about their security in old-age are compared with similar information from studies conducted in Maharashtra state of India and Thailand. They are presented in Table 8.9. From the Table it is evident that most of the parents in Dakshina Kannada district of Karnataka State, like the parents of Thailand expect support (financial or otherwise) from their children in old age. In Maharashtra State of India, a large proportion of men aged 25-59 (53 per cent) who were optimistic about their old age indicated that they felt so because sons will provide them security. While in Thailand nearly 50 per cent of husbands mentioned savings, pensions, help from family and charity as other sources of support in old-age, in Dakshina Kannada district of India, the number of women mentioning these sources is only about 25 per cent of the total respondents.

Data collected for this study give us some insight into old age security realized by parents in rural India. Adapting the method followed by Nag and others (1978) we have examined the residential pattern of 103 aged (60+) persons who account for 5 per cent of the total population, as those who are staying with sons (daughters-in-law and their children if any), with sons and daughters (their spouses and children, if any) and with others. We have also examined the work participation rate and the work status of the aged by residential pattern. Admittedly the sample size of the aged is very small for any meaningful indepth analysis. A comparative picture of the residential pattern of the aged in the villages of Dakshina Kannada district of Karnataka State of India, Nepal and Java are given in Table 8.10.

TABLE 8.9: **Parents' Expectation of Old Age Support from Children**

India					
Rural Dakshina Kannada district of Karnataka State			*Rural Maharashtra State*		
Responses (women aged 90-45)	*Percentages*		*Responses (Reasons for optimistic attitude in old age by men aged (25-59)*	*Percentages*	
1. Financial help expected from children	80.10	N=211	1. Sons will provide security	53.00	N=143
2. Financial help expected from other sources	24.65		2. Income sufficient from land/ business	37.00	
3. Expectation to live with adult children in future	85.78		3. Can't say	10.00	
4. Expectation to live with adult children only in old age	25.41	N=181			
5. Expectation to live with adult children throughout life	74.03				

Thailand		
Responses (Husbands)	Petcentage	
1. Expectation of old age support from children	75.50	N=2967
2. Expectation of old age support from savings, pension or social security help from family and charity	49.60	
3. A great deal of financial support expected from children	27.70	N=2958
4. No financial support expected from children	11.80	
5. Expectation to live with children in old age	84.20	N=2960

Sources: 1. Field data.

2. (Vlassoff M. and Vlassoff C., 1980: 493).

3. (Arnold F. and Chiniana P., 1977: 10-12).

TABLE 8.10: **Residential Pattern of the Aged**

Residence of the aged	*Dakshina Kannada district of Karnataka State of India*	*Java (Indonesia)*	*Nepal*
	N=103	*N=121*	*N=180*
1. Staying with son (daughter-in-law and their children if any)	44 (42.72)	32 (26.45)	88 (48.89)
2. Staying with daughter (son-in-law and their children, if any)	5 (4.85)	36 (29.75)	19 (10.56)
3. Staying with son and daughter (their spouses and children, if any)	49 (47.57)	20 (16.53)	23 (12.78)
4. Staying with others than mentioned above (including staying alone)	5 (4.85)	33 (27.27)	50 (27.78)

Note : Figures in parentheses refer to the percentage distribution.

Sources: Column 1 Field data
Columns 2 and 3 : (Nag *et al*., 1978 : 299-300).

About 95 per cent of the aged in Dakshina Kannada district stay with their children. Out of them, 40 per cent stay with their sons alone. Though aged parents usually stay with their children, most of the aged males were reported to be working. But the term 'work participation' has a broader connotation in the sense that it is inclusive of both who are "willingly working" without any monetary motivation and those who are "forced to work" for monetary benefits. In the present context, these two distinguishable terms have to be borne in mind, for, those who are willingly working are doing so not because they do not get adequate support from their children, but may be to keep themselves away from boredom at home. It is found that 78 per cent of the aged working men who are staying with their children are family workers.

They are those who own land and they may be possibly working in a supervisory capacity.

With regard to the aged who are staying 'with others' (including those who are staying with daughters and their spouses and children, if any) nearly 80 per cent of males and 40 per cent of females were found to be working. Out of them 50 per cent of the aged males and 100 per cent of the aged females were found to be other than family workers (other than family workers including employees and single workers). When the work status of the aged who are staying with their sons is compared to the work status of the aged who are staying 'with others' than sons it implicitly shows that the latter work with the primary intention of direct monetary benefits.

9

COMPENDIUM AND CONCLUDING REMARKS

9.1 Compendium

Past work on fertility has taken into account the role of children as an element in fertility decision-making of couples. Some of the studies on economic activities of children have shown that child labour significantly contributes to the household production. But in the specific setting of India, only a few fragmentary pieces of evidence are available on this topic. Hence the present study has been designed to focus on the economic activities of children in the Indian context in a greater detail. It has been an attempt at explaining the dimensions, causes and consequences of child work participation in the rural areas. The overall objective of the study is, of course, to assess the economic contribution of children to the household economy. The specific objectives, however, are:

1. to study the participation of children in economic activities at home and outside home in terms of (a) the magnitude of work, (b) the intensity of work, (c) the place of work, (d) the nature of activities performed. and (e) the wages earned;
2. to study the compatibility and/or competitiveness of work and schooling of children in rural situations;
3. to identify the causes of child work participation in rural areas;

4. to highlight some of the consequences of child work participation; and
5. to understand parents' perceptions of the importance of economic contribution of children.

A detailed review of available literature on the topic was carried out initially, to get a better insight into the problem. The review threw up some important issues around which the discussion in the study is centered. These issues are:

(a) Do children combine schooling and work? If so, do they form a significant proportion?
(b) If a significant proportion of children are combining schooling and work, do the magnitude, intensity and the nature of work performed by them and the wages earned or their tangible contribution vary significantly from those who do not combine work with schooling?
(c) What are the major factors which determine child work participation?

The investigation began with an analysis of available secondary data. The secondary data analysis gave some hints on the dimensions and some of the causes of child work participation in the rural areas. The need for primary investigation was, however, deeply felt in the Indian context, mainly due to the paucity of data from secondary sources especially on work-school status of children. Taking note of these requirements, data were collected from three villages of Dakshina Kannada district by using pre-tested interview schedules.

For purpose of analysis children (6-15) were grouped into four mutually exclusive categories according to their work-school status. Thus each child in the sample was categorised into one of the following categories: (1) those who go to school but do not work; (2) those who go to school and also work; (3) those who work but do not go to school; and (4) those who neither work nor go to school. This classification showed that children who combined schooling with work made up a significant proportion (26 per cent of boys and 17 per cent of girls) though not the largest proportion in the child population of 6-15 years. Bulk of marginal child workers fell in this category who were overlooked in the census count. Similarly, children who neither worked nor attended school also formed a significant proportion in the child population by making up 20 per cent of boys and 26 per cent of girls. Most of them were found in the lower age group of 6-8 years. As they entered higher ages they moved out of this category either by attending school or by participating in work. Some of them who enrolled themselves in schools gradually dropped out from schools and became full-fledged workers.

Schooling was found to be compatible with work by working after school hours and/or during school vacation. Beedi rolling activity and to some extent farming activities could be easily combined with schooling both by way of working out-of-school hours and during school vacation. Though compatibility of work and schooling was found to be easier by engaging in beedi rolling activities, the highest concentration of workers who did not attend school was also found in this industry. In situations where work and schooling were competitive, child work intensity was comparatively higher than in situations where work and schooling were compatible.

More than one half of children in the school-going age group did engage themselves in household duties. In the category of those who neither worked nor went to school, nearly 60 per cent of boys and 43 per cent of girls were not even participating in household chores. They were absolutely idle. Among household duties the highest participation of children of both the sexes was found in carrying water for household consumption.

For purpose of analysing the causes of child work participation, a bivariate classification of children was made by taking the percentage distribution of children in each work-school status category across background variables. The background variables were selected on an *a priori* basis. Chi-square test was used to show the statistical significance of the associatian.

An inverse relationship was hypothesized between household income and child work participation. But the results showed that the inverse relationship might start operating only after some threshold level of income was reached. Between household income and idleness rate of children, a well pronounced negative relationship was observed. On the other hand, increase in income boosted up the number of full-time school attending children. Possession of more land improved schooling rate and increased the work participation rate of boys. Possession of land also facilitated children to combine schooling and work which, however, resulted in lower intensity of work.

The highest work participation rates and schooling rates were found among those household having more number of siblings. Encouragement to the younger siblings by the participation of their elder ones in school or work seemed to be the reason for this pattern. Positive association between number of siblings and work intensity of children was also observed in the study. Presence of educated adult members in the family improved the schooling rate of children and brought down their idleness rate. Schooling rate varied directly with caste hierarchy. It was found to be higher among Hindus than among Muslims. Household industries like beedi rolling encouraged Muslim females as well in labour force as it could be performed within the household. Nevertheless, very high idleness rate of children among Muslims was noticed. Similarly, higher idleness rate was found among Scheduled Castes and Scheduled Tribes also.

Availability of and distance to high school seemed to influence the schooling rate of children. Non-availability of schools in the native village increased the cost of education which in turn discouraged parents from sending their children to school. This in many cases lead to higher child work participation.

Child work participation was found to have affected the performance of children in the school, especially when work was combined with schooling by worki g out-of-school hours. Poor performance in the school by working children has an implication on their slow mental development. However, in terms of work-input, their contribution was felt very useful by the parents. In areas where child work participation was higher, levels of fertility appeared to be high. In wage earning activities children's participation seemed to discourage the employment of adults. Those who performed household duties seemed to encourage mothers' participation in labour force.

The analysis of parents' perception of work and old-age security utility of children brought out some important findings. Majority of parents perceived some help in the activities that the children performed at home and outside home. They also perceived children as the major source of financial support in their old age. They expected to live with their children even when their children were grown up and married.

A minimum of secondary education was emphasized by parents for their children irrespective of sex. Expenses incurred in sending children for higher level of education appeared to be the main factor discouraging parents to plan for their children's education. Though not the main reason, the support which parents expected from their children also emerged as an important factor which might deprive the children of higher education. A large number of parents expect their children to start helping their family economically before they crossed their eighth year of life. Regarding parents' realization of support in old age, it was found that about 95 per cent of parents lived with their children in their old age.

We may now round off the findings of the present study by way of presenting answers to the questions raised in the beginning. Unlike the studies made so far, our study does not merely suggest a simplistic dichotomy of working and school-going children; there are children who combine work and schooling, and their proportion is not insignificant. The magnitude, intensity and the nature of activities performed by these children and the wages earned by them vary markedly from those who do not combine schooling and work. The study also indicated that factors like caste/religion, possession of cultivable land, income, sibling number, age of the child, school facility, etc. determine the participation of children in work, through their schooling status, in terms of both magnitude and intensity of work in the rural areas.

What are the theoretical and policy implications of the

above findings? While we recognize that there is need for mustering a vast amount of data and for conducting a large number of similar micro studies to draw conclusive and study implications it is attempted to look at what our findings would mean to theory and policy. This is done in the final section of the thesis which follows.

9.2 Concluding Remarks

The discussion on the micro-theory of fertility pivots on the utility of children to their parents. It has been argued that this has a relationship with the fertility decision-making of couples. According to the theory, the economic and security utility of children outweigh the cost of their upbringing in developing societies. The economic and security utility could be analysed in terms of the current and future utility. The current utility comprises of the economic benefits children render by working at home and outside home and the physical security they provide to their parents when they are disabled. The future utility would be in the form of financial, residential and physical support that the children provide to their parents in their old age.

The current and future utility of children vary by their work-school status, for, the magnitude and intensity of work, the nature of activities performed and the wages earned and contributed to the family income by children vary by their work-school status. In the case of those who go to school but do not work, the current utility is the discounted value of their future utility. Of course, these children are found to be participating and spending some time in household duties which probably is the minimum work utility every rural parent derives from their children when they cross certain age level. About 32 per cent of boys and 35 per cent of girls who participate in household duties in this category put in about 45 man-days of work for performing these activities. This category of schooling children who do not perform any activity other than putting-in some hours for household duties, if allowed to continue their education would be maximising their future income utility to their parents at the cost of their current work and income utility. But, on the other hand, those who work and do not attend school maximise their current work or income utility or both by discounting their future income utility. Those who earn wages among them contribute substantially to their family income. These children are the ones who give maximum current income utility to their parents. Others in this category who do not participate in wage labour but put in more time to work so as to help their parents besides helping them in household duties also render perceivably high work utility to their parents. A cursory look at Table 6.5 reveals the high work-input by this category of children.

As mentioned earlier children who combine schooling and work form a significantly large proportion of the child population. No doubt, they participate in work and perform household duties but their work intensity in terms of man-days worked is comparatively lower (Table 6.5). This is because of their limited disposable time to work due to school attendance. But combination of schooling and work retards their progress in the school which may ultimately result in drop-out from school. Those who pull out from work force and continue education maximise their future income utility. Many among those who do not, improve their current utility by dropping out from the school.

Children falling in the category of 'neither working nor attending school' render minimum current and future utility to their parents. Their current utility is in the form of help in household activities. But all of them do not perform household chores. Of course, nearly 67 per cent of girls and 40 per cent of boys of this category who participate in household chores spend the highest number of man-days for these activities. The future utility of children belonging to this cotegory like those who work and do not go to school will be minimum compared to those who attend school, if education could be taken as a factor that improves their future income utility.

Higher education could improve in most of the cases, only the future income but not the future non-income utility, *viz.* the residence they provide and the physical support they render to the parents during old age. Education leads to search for better jobs which in turn leads to moving out to cities and isolation from parents. Of course, most of these migrant children send remittances to their parents (Population Reports, 1983: M-261).

The above conclusions on the utility of children have implications on the fertility decision making of couples. If work and income utility of children as main components of their current utility have a major role to play in the fertility decision-making of couples in the rural areas then the fertility rates among those couples whose children belong to the categories of 'attending school and no work' and 'no work and no school' are expected to be lower. Among those whose children belong to the categories of 'combining schooling and work' and 'working and not attending school', the fertility rate is expected to be comparatively higher. Of course, here we presume that the decision making of parents to have subsequent children depends upon their perception of work, income and security utility which they are going to derive from them and that their perceptions do not vary significantly from their realization. In other words, the belongingness of children in any of these categories based on work-school status was rightly perceived by their parents at the time of their fertility decision-making.

Parents who perceive and realize minimum current utility from their children do not necessarily belong to the upper socio-economic strata of the society alone. They are from among the poor also. In other words, it is a wrong notion that parents from all the poor households perceive and realize high work and income utility from their children. Those children who do not have any household assets to work and do not find any work in the labour market could render only the minimum current utility to their parents. This study showed that majority of those who 'neither work nor go to school' belonged to the poorest section of the society. On the other hand those who 'attend school but do not work' belonged to the upper strata of the society (Table 7.1). In both the cases the current utility of children is minimum. Hence it is not correct to say that poor households perceive high economic value of children. In areas where the proportion of children who neither work nor attend school is large, reciprocally one may find the perception of large number of parents of the economic utility of their children turning out to be very low. This conclusion does not imply that current economic value of children to their parents, in rural areas, is very low. Therefore, economic value of children to their parents should not be studied in isolation but it should be analysed in the light of the conditions which determine them.

Schooling emerged as an important factor determining the current utility of children to their parents. School attendance either brings down the work participation rate or reduces their work intensity. In other words, it minimises the current utility of children which has an implication of fertility decision-making of parents. Therefore, any policy measures towards universalisation of school education will influence first the work intensity and gradually the work participation of children thereby reducing their current utility to their parents. But the effect of the universalisation of education on child work participation and child work intensity will not be immediate and certainly will not be total, for, the degree of influence will vary across socio-economic groups. The response towards universalisation of education will be determined by other socio-economic variables such as income, caste, literacy level of the decision-makers in the households, etc. In many cases child work participation itself deter children's responsiveness towards universalisation of education. Therefore, much has to be done to increase the responsiveness of different socio-economic groups towards compulsory primary education. If that is done, one could foresee a situation at least in the long run where current utility of children to their parents is on the lower side and the future utility on the higher.

Any policy measures to improve the schooling rate of children in the rural areas should take into account the current economic utility of children to their parents discounted for the future. The opportunity cost of schooling of the child, therefore, is the direct and indirect contributions of children to the household economy which the parents forego. If that is compensated parents may not find any reasons to detain their children for work. Compensation could be in cash or kind to the parents of school going children. But if compensation is given for all school going children of the family the inducement will be for a higher fertility and a larger family size. Hence an eligibility criterion need to be arrived at for paying compensation by laying down the specification for the number of children a parent should have. Since the national family planning programmes are for a 'two children norm' "every child who does not have more than one sibling" could be taken as the eligibility criterion. Poor households could be defined in terms of annual family income. The compensation paid for school going children of the poor households, for the income they forego by being at school should be decided by way of assessing the average annual contribution of a child to the household economy in different socio-economic situations. Over and above the compensation paid for foregoing the economic contribution of the two children, an additional compensation for not having more than two children should be given to the parents which should make up for the net economic remittances parents forego by restricting their off-spring number to two. The prescribed scheme should, thus, help towards achieving the twin objectives, *viz.* retarding fertility rate and bringing down the incidence of child labour if not in terms of participation rate at least in terms of child work intensity, in the long run.

BIBLIOGRAPHY

Ahuja K., 1978, *Idle Labour in Village India*, New Delhi, Manohar.

Arles J.P., 1971, "The Economic and Social Promotion of Scheduled Castes and Scheduled Tribes", *International Labour Review*, Vol. 103, No. 2.

Arnold F., *et al*, 1975, *The Value of Children : Introduction and Comparative Analysis*, Honalulu, East West Centre.

Arnold F. and P. Chintana, 1977, *Economic Factors in Family Size Decisions in Thailand*, Institute of Population Studies, Chulalonkoran University, Bangkok.

Bardhan P. K., 1970, "On the Minimum Level of Living and the Rural Poor, *Indian Economic Review*, Vol. 5.

Becker G.S., 1960, "An Economic Analysis of Fertility", in National Bureau of Economic Research (ed.), *Demographic and Economic Change in Developed Countries*, Princeton, Princeton University Press.

——, 1965, "A Theory of the Allocation of Time", *Economic Journal*, Vol. 75, No. 299, pp. 493-517.

Becker G.S., and H.G. Lewis, 1973, "On the Interaction between the Quantity and Quality of Children", *Journal of Political Economy*, Vol. 81, No. 2, Suppl. pp. 279-288.

Ben-Porath Y., 1970, "*Fertility in Israel—An Economists' Interpretation : Differentials and Trends*, 1950-1970, RM-5981-FF, Santa Monica, (California), Rand Corp.

——, 1973, "Economic Analysis of Fertility in Israel : Point and Counterpoint", *Journal of Political Economy*, Vol. 81, No. 2, Suppl, pp. 202-233.

——, 1974, "Notes on the Micro-economics of Fertility",

International Social Science Journal, Vol. 26, No. 2, pp. 302-314.

Berelson B., 1973, "The Value of Children : Taxonomical Essay", *Population Council Annual Report* (1972), New York, Population Council, pp. 19-27.

Bertrand A.L., 1958, *Rural Sociology : An Analysis of Contemporary Rural Life*, London, McGraw Hill Book Company.

Bhatty I.Z., 1974, "Inequality and Poverty in Rural India", in T.N. Srinivasan and P.K. Bardhan (ed.), *Poverty and Income Distribution in India*, Calcutta, Statistical Publishing Society.

Blake, J., 1967, "Income and Reproduction Motivation", *Population Studies*, Vol. 21, No. 3, pp. 185-206.

——— 1968, "Are Babies Consumer Durable?", *Population* Studies, Vol. 22, No. 1, pp. 5-25.

Blake, J., 1971, "Reproductive Motivation and Population Policy", *Bio-Science*, Vol. 21, No. 5, pp. 215-220.

Bulato A.R., and F. Arnold, 1977, "Relationship Between the Value and Cost of Children and Fertility : Cross Cultural Evidence", *International Population Conference*, Mexico (1977), Vol. 1, IUSSP, pp. 141-156.

Buripkadi, C., 1977, "*The Value of Children—A Cross National Study of Thailand*, Vol. 4, East West Centre, Honalulu and the Institute for Population Studies, Bangkok, Chululongkaran University.

Cain M.T., 1977, "The Economic Activities of Children in a Village in Bangladesh", *Population and Development Review*, Vol. 3, No. 3, pp. 201-229.

Caldwell J.C., 1967, "Fertility Attitudes in Three Economically Contrasting Rural Regions of Ghana", *Economic Development and Cultural Change*, Vol. 15, No. 2, Part 1, pp. 217-238.

——, 1976 a, "Toward a Restatement of Demographic Transition Theory", *Population and Development Review*, Vol. 2, No. 3 & 4, pp. 321-366.

——, 1976 b, "*The Socio-economic Explanation of High Fertility*, Canberra, Australian National University.

——, 1977, "The Economic Rationality of High Fertility ;

An InvestigationIllustrated with Nigerian Data", *Population Studies*, Vol. 31, No. 1, pp. 5-27.

Chung B.J., 1972, "Costs and Benefits of Children in Hong Kong : Measurement in a Pilot Study", in Fawcett (ed.), *The Satisfactions and Costs of Children : Theories, Concepts, Methods*, pp. 210-230.

Cochrane S.H., 1975, "Children as By-products, Investment Goods and Consumer Goods : A Review of Some Micro-Economic Models of Fertility", *Population Studies*. Vol. 29, No. 3, pp. 373-390.

Correa J.P., 1979, "Child in Asia—UNESCO Statement", *Child in Third World*, New Delhi, People's Publishing House.

Davangzo J., 1972, *The Determinants of Family Formation in Chile, 1960 : An Econometric Study of Female Labour Force Participation, Marriage and Fertility Decisions*, A Report prepared for International Development, Santa Monica, (California), Rand Corporation.

Davis K., 19'/0, "Population Policy : Will Current Programmes Succeed?" in Ashish Bose *et al* (ed.), *Studies in Demography*, pp. 369-398, First Published in *Science*, 158, November 10, 1967, pp. 730-739.

Demeny P., 1972, "Economic Approaches to the Value of Children : An Overview" in Fawcett (ed.) *The Statisfactions and Costs of Children : Theories, Concepts, Methods*, pp. 17-23.

Detray D. N., 1972, *The Interaction Between Parent Investment in Children and Family Size : An Econometric Analysis*, R-1003-RF, *Santa Monica*, (California), Rand Corporation.

——, 1973, "Child Quality and the Demand for Children", *Journal of Political Economy*, Vol. 81, No. 2, Supplement, pp. 70-95.

Easterlin R.A., 1969, "Towards a Socio-Economic Theory of Fertility : A Survey of Recent Research on Economic Factors in American Fertility" in S.J. Behrman *et al*, (ed.), *Fertility and Family Planning : A World Review*, Ann Arbor, University of Michigan Press, pp. 127-156.

——, 1972, "The Economics and Sociology of Fertility :

A Synthesis", *Paper Prepared for Seminar on Early Industrialisation*, Princeton.

Espenshade T.J , 1972, "The Price of Children and Socio-Economic Theories of Fertility", *Population Studies*, Vol. 26, No. 2, pp. 207-221.

——, 1977, "The Value and Cost of Children", *Population Bulletin*, Population Council, Vol. 32, No. 1.

Fawcett J.T., (ed.), 1972, *The Satisfactions and Costs of Children : Theories, Concepts, Methods*, Honalulu, East-West Centre.

——, 1973, *Psychological Perspectives on Population*, New York, Basic Books.

——, 1978, "Value and Costs of Children to Parents", *Proceedings of the International Population Conference*, Mexico (1977), IUSSP, pp. 171-179.

Freedman R., 1973, "Norms for Family Size in Underdeveloped Areas", in Micklin (ed.), *Environment and Social Organisation: Current Issues in Human Ecology*, Illinois, The Dryden Press.

Gordon D.M., 1972, *Theories of Poverty and Unemployment*, Heath, Lexington Books.

Ghosh B., 1975, "Recent Studies in Social and Economic Determinants of Fertility: A Review and Critique", *Journal of Family Welfare*, Vol. 21, No. 3, pp. 38-45.

Government of India, Ministry of Labour, 1965, *Rural Labour Enquiry, 1963-65*, Final Report, Simla.

——, Ministry of Education, 1962, *Education in India: 1958-59*, Delhi, Manager of Publications.

——, 1977, *The Education Quarterly*, Vol. 29, No. 2.

——, 1980, *Enrolment Trends in States: 1968-69 to 1978-79*, Delhi, Controller of Publications.

——, Ministry of Labour, 1979, *Report of the Committee on Child Labour*, Delhi, The Controller of Publications.

Government of Karnataka, 1980, *Karnataka Draft Sixth Five Year Plan 1980-85*, Bangalore, Planning Department.

Goddard V. and B. White, 1982, "Child Workers and Capitalist Development: An Introductory Note and Bibliography", *Development and Change*, Vol. 13, No. 4, pp. 465.477.

Gronau R., 1973, "The Effects of Children on the Housewife's Value of Time", *Journal of Political Economy*, Vol. 81, No. 2, Supplement, pp. 200-201.

Harman, A.J., 1970, *Fertility and Economic Behaviour of Families in the Philippines*, RM-6385—AID, Santa Monica (California), Rand Corporation.

Harper E.B., 1970, "A Comparative Analysis of Caste: The United States and India", in Milton Singer and Bernard S. Cohn (ed.), *Structure and Change in Indian Society*, Chicago, Aldino Publishing Company.

Hoffman L.W., and M.L. Hoffman, 1973, "The Value of Children to Parents", in J.T. Fawcett (ed.), *Psychological Perspectives on Population*, Basic Books, New York, pp. 19-76.

Hull T., 1975, *Each Child Brings Its Own Fortune: An Enquiry into the Value of Children in a Japanese Village*, Unpublished Ph. D. Dissertation, Canberra, Australian National University.

——, 1977, "The Influence of Social Class on the Need and Effective Demand for Children in a Japanese Village", in Lado T. Ruzicka (ed), *The Economic and Social Supports for High Fertility*, Proceedings of the Conference held in Canberra (16-18 November), 1976, Canberra, Australian National University, pp. 307-318.

Hull T.J. and V.J. Hull, 1977, "The Relation of Economic Class and Fertility: An Analysis of Some Indonesian Data", *Population Studies*, Vol. 31, No. 1, pp. 43-57.

Hull V.J., 1976, *The Positive Relation Between Economic Class and Family Size in Java*, Population Institute, Yogjakarta, Gadjah Mada University.

Hull V., 1977, "Social and Ecocomic Supports for High Fertility in Peasant Communities: General Issues Emerging from Specific Research", in Lado T. Ruzica (ed.), *The Economic and Social Supports for High Fertility*, Canberra, Australian National University, pp. 241-250.

Jose A.V., 1974, "Trends in Real Wage Rates of Agricultural Labourers", *Economic and Political Weekly*, Vol. 9, No. 3.

Ketkar S.V., 1979, *History of Caste in India*, Rawat Publications, Jaipur.

Krishnaji N., 1971, "Wages of Agricultural Labour", *Economic and Political Weekly*, Vol. 6, No. 39.

Kulshrestha J.C., 1978, *Child Labour in India*, New Delhi, Ashish Publishing House.

Kulkarni S., 1979, "Economic Value of Children", in K. Srinivasan *et al* (ed.), *Demographic and Socio-economic Aspects of the Child in India*, Bombay, Himalaya Publishing House, pp. 234-252

Leibenstein H., 1957, *Economic Backwardness and Economic Growth*, New York, Wiley, London.

——, 1974 a, "An Interpretation of the Economic Theory of Fertility—Promising Path or Blind Alley?", *Journal of Economic Literature*, Vol. 12, No. 2, pp. 457-479.

——, 1974 b, "Relation of Economic Development to Fertility", in Leon Tabah (ed.), *Population Growth and Economic Development in the Third World*, Vol. II, Dolhian Belgium, Ordina Editions, pp. 473-508.

Madigan F., 1977, "Decline from High Fertility in Western Misamis Oriental: Interpretation of a Philippine Case History", in Lado T. Ruzicka (ed.), *The Economic and Social Supports for High Fertility*, Canberra, Australian National University, pp. 275-286.

Mamdani M., 1972, *The Myth of Population Control: Family, Caste and Class in an Indian Village*, New York, Monthly Review Press.

Mandelbaum D.G., 1972, *Society in India*, Vol. 1, Bombay, Popular Prakashan.

Mehryas A.H., *et al*, 1977, "Changing Perception of Children's Value and Cost by Groups of Parents in an Iranian City : Report on an on-going Project". In Lado T. Ruzicka (ed.), *The Economic and Social Supports for High Fertility*, Canberra, Australian National University, pp. 423-438.

Mellor J.W., 1976, *The New Economics of Growth: A Strategy for India and the Developing World*, London, Cornell University Press.

Mendelvich E., 1979, "Child Labour", *International Labour Review*, Vol. 118, No. 5.

Mincer J., 1963, "Market Prices, Opportunity Costs and Income Effects", in Carl F. Christ (ed.), *Measurement in Economics: Studies in Mathematical Economics ann Econometrics in Memory of Yehuda Grunfeld*, Stanford, Stanford University Press, pp. 67-82.

Minhas B.S., 1970, "Rural Poverty, Land Distribution and Development", *Indian Economic Review*, Vol. 5.

Mitra A., 1970, "The Small Family Norm and Literaey", in Ashish Bose, *et al* (ed.), *Studies in Demography*, pp. 290-300.

Mueller E., 1972 a, Economic Cost and Value of Children: Conceptualisation and Measurement", in Fawcett (ed.), *The Satisfaction and Costs of Children: Theories, Concepts, Methods*, Honalulu, East-West Centre, pp. 174-205.

Mueller E., 1976, "The Economic Value of Children in Peasant Agriculture", in Ronald G. Ridker (ed), *Population and Development: The Search for Selective Interventions*, Baltimore, John Hopkins University Press, pp. 98-153.

Murthy K.R. and C.R. Rao, 1979, "Economic Rationality of Reproduction Motivation: A case study of Jalaris of Vishakapattanam Town", in K. Srinivasan *et al* (ed.), *D mographic and Socio-economic aspects of the Child in India*, Bombay, Himalaya Publishing House, pp. 253-272.

Myrdal G., 1968, *Asian Drama: An Enquiry into the Poverty of Nations*, Vol. I, II and III, USA, Penguin Books.

Nadkarni M.V., 1976, "Over Population and Rural Poor", *Economic and Political Weekly*, Vol. 2, No. 31 and 32, pp. 1163-1172.

Nag M., 1972 a, "Economic Value of Children in Agriculture Societies: Evaluation of Existing Knowledge and an Anthropological Approach", in Fawcett (ed.), *The Satisfactions and Costs of Children: Theories, Concepts, Methods*, Honalulu, East-West Centre, pp. 58-93.

——, 1972 b, *Factors Affecting Human Fertility in Non-Industrialized Societies. A Cross-cultural Study*, New Haven, Yale University.

——, 1975, *Economic Cost and Value of Children in Javanese, Nepalese and Peruvian villages*, Contract NICHD-71-2209 (Final Report), International Institute for the Study of Human Reproduction, New Kork, Columbia University.

Nag M., *et al*, 1977, "Economic Value of Children in Two Peasant Societies", *International Population Conference, Mexico*, Vol. 1, Leige, IUSSP.

——, 1978, "An Anthropological Approach to the Study of the Economic Value of Children in Java and Nepal", *Current Anthropology*, Vol. 19, No. 2, pp. 293-306.

Namboodiri N.K., 1972, "Some Observations on the Economic Framework of Fertility Analysis", *Population Studies*, Vol. 26, No. 2, pp. 185-206.

Nerlove M. and T.P. Schultz, 1970, *Love and Life Between the Censuses: A Model of Family Decision Making in Purito Rico, 1950-60*, Santa Monica (California), Rand Corporation.

Okore A, 1977, "The Rationale for High Fertility in Rural Nigeria: The case of the Ibos of Arochukwa in Two States of Nigeria", in Lado T. Ruzicka (ed.), *The Economic and Social Supports for High Fertility*, Canberra, Australian National University, pp. 253-274.

Oppong C., 1973, *Growing up in Dagbon*, Accra, Ghana Publishing Company.

Peek P., 1978, "The Education and Employment of Children: A Comparative Study of Sansalvador and Khartoum", in Guy Standing and Glen Seehan (ed.), *Labour Force Participation in Low Income Countries*, Geneva, ILO, pp. 177-190.

Population Reports, 1983, *Series M., No.* 7, USA, John Hopkins Press.

Population Reference Bureau, 1979, *World Children Data Sheet*, Washington DC.

Poston D.L. and J. Singlemann, 1975, "Socio-Economic Status, Value Orientations and Fertility Behaviour in India", *Demography*, Vol. 12, No. 3, pp. 417-430.

Premi M.K., "Student workers in the Age Group 5-14: A Socio-Demographic Analysis", *Manpower Journal*, Vol. 8, No. 4.

Radhadevi, 1978, *Fertility Performance of Working Women in Trivandrum District: A Case Study*, Unpublished Thesis for Doctoral Degree, Submitted to the University of Mysore.

Rao *et al*., 1986, *Determinants of Fertility Decline: A Study of Rural Karnataka*, South Asian Publishers, New Delhi.

Rayappa P.H., and D. Grover, 1980. *Employment Planning for the Rural Poor—The Case of Scheduled Castes and Scheduled Tribes*, New Delhi, Sterling Publishers Private Limited.

Repetto R.J., 1976, "Direct Economic Cost and Value of Children", in Ronald G. Ridker (ed.), *Population and Development: The Search for Selective Interventions*, Maryland, Baltimore, Johns Hopkins University Press.

Reyna S.P., 1975, "Pronatalism and Child Labour: Chadian Attitudes to Birth Control and Family Size" in J.C. Caldwell (ed.), *Population Growth and Socio-Economic Change in West Africa*, New York, Columbia University Press, pp. 582-591.

Rodgers G., and G.Standing, 1981, "Economic Roles of Children in Low Income Countries", *International Labour Review*, Vol. 120, No. 1.

Rosenzweig M.R., 1975, "The Demand for Children in Farm Households", *Journal of Political Economy*, Vol. 85. No. 1, pp. 123-146.

Rosenzweig M.R., and R. Evenson, 1977, "Fertility, Schooling and the Economic Contribution of Children in Rural India: An Econometric Analysis", *Econometrica*, Vol. 45, No. 5, pp. 1065-1079.

Ruzicka L.T. (ed.), 1977, *The Economic and Social Supports for High Fertility, Proceedings of the Conference in Canberra (1976)*, Canberra, Australian National University Printing Service.

Sarma M.T.R., 1977, *Economic Value of Children in Rural India*, Centre Discussion Paper, No. 272, Economic Growth Centre, Yale University.

Sau, R., 1971, "On Rural Poverty: A Tentative Hypothesis", *Economic and Political Weekly*, Vol. 6, No. 52, pp. 2563-2564.

Sawhney N., 1979, "Occupational Pattern of children in Rural Uttar Pradesh", in K. Srinivasan *et al* (ed.), *Demographic and Socio-economic Aspects of the Child in India*, Bombay, Himalaya Publishing House.

Schultz T.P., 1970, *Fertility Patterns and Their Determinants in the Arab Middle East*, RN-5978, FF, Santa Monica, (California). Rand Corporation.

——, 1971, "An Economic Perspective on Population Growth", *Rapid Population Growth: Consequences and Policy Implications*, Vol. 2, Baltimore, Johns Hopkins University Press, pp. 148-174.

Schultz T.W., 1973, "The Economic Value of Children: An Economic Perspective", *Journal of Political Economy*, Vol. 81, No. 2, Supplement, pp. 2-13.

——, 1974, "Fertility and Economic Values" in Theodore W. Schultz (ed.), *Economics of the Family: Marriage, Children and Human Capital*, Chicago, University of Chicago Press, pp. 3-22.

Senart E., 1975, *Caste in India: The Facts and Systems*, Delhi, ESSESS Publications.

Sen A.K., 1974, "Poverty, Inequality and Unemployment: Some Conceptual Issues", in T.N. Srinivasan and P.K. Bardhan (ed.), *Poverty and Income Distribution in India*, Calcutta, Statistical Publishing Society.

Shortlidge R.L., 1976, *A Socio-Economic Model of School Attendance*, Cornell Agricultural Economics, Occasional Paper No. 86 (Mimeo).

Sills D.L. (ed.), 1972, *International Encyclopaedia of Social Sciences*, Vol. II, USA, Collier and Macmillan Inc.

Simon J.L., 1969, "The Effect of Income on Fertility", *Population Studies*, Vol. 23, No. 3, pp. 327-341.

Simons A.B., 1977, "The Value of Children Approach in Population Policies, A New Hope or False Promise?", *International Population Conference, Mexico (1977)*, Vol. 1, IUSSP, Liege, pp. 157-180.

Synder D.W., 1974, "Economic Determinants of Family Size in Western Africa, *Demography*, Vol. II, No. 4, pp. 613-628.

Srikantan K.S., *et al*, 1978, *Female and Child Work Participation in Integrated Development of a Command Area*, Bangalore, Institute for Social and Economic Change.

Suchart P., 1977, "Cost and Value of Children in Rural Thailand", in Lado T. Ruzicka (ed.), *The Economic and Social Supports for High Fertility*, Canberra, Australian National University, pp. 307-318.

Turner J, 1974, "Economic Context and the Meaning of Children to parents in Chile", *Paper Presented at Second International Conference of the Association for Cross Cultural Psychology*, Kingston, Ontario, August 1974 (Mimeo).

Turchi B.A., 1975, "Micro-Economic Theories of Fertility: A Critique", *Social Forces*, Vol 54, No. 1, pp. 107-138.

United Nations, 1968, *Methods of Analysing Census Data on Economic Activities of the Population*, Population Studies, No. 43, New York, UN Publications.

United Nations, 1973, *The Determinants and Consequences of Population Trends*, Vol. 1, New York,

Vlassoff M., 1979, "Labour Demand and Economic Utility—A Case Study in Rural India," *Population Studies*, Vol. 33, No. 3, pp. 415-428.

Vlassoff M., and C. Vlassoff, 1980, "Old Age Security and Utility of Children in Rural India", *Population Studies*, Vol. 34, No. 2.

White B., 1975, "The Economic Importance of Children in a Javanese Village", in Moni Nag (ed.), *Population and Social Organisation*, Hague, Paris, Mounton Publishers.

White B., 1976, *Production and Reproduction in a Javanese Village*. Unpublisned Ph.D. dissertation, Columbia University.

Willis R.J., 1973, "A New Approach to the Economic Theory of Fertility Behaviour", *Journal of Political Economy*, Vol. 81, No. 2, Supplement, pp. 14-64.

Willis R.J., 1974, "Economic Theory of Fertility Behaviour", in TW Schultz (ed), *Economics of the Family*, Chicago, Chicago Press, pp. 25-75.

Wong A.K., 1977, "The Value of Children and the Household Economy in an Urban Setting: A Review of Current VOC Studies in the Developing World", in Lado T. Ruzicka (ed), *The Economic and Social Supports of High Fertility*, Canberra, Australian National University, pp. 319-344.

Wyon J.W., and J.E. Gordon, 1971, *The Khanna Study of Population Problems in the Rural Punjab* (*India*), Cambridge (Massachusetts), Harvard University Press.

Zachariah K.C., and B.L. Newlon, 1983, *A Comparative Analysis of the Determinants of Fertility Decline in Sri Lanka and South India*, The World Bank.

INDEX